CAMBRIDGE
UNIVERSITY PRESS

CAMBRIDGE ENGLI
Language Assessment
Part of the University of Cambridge



# Kid's Box

Updated
Second Edition

## Teacher's Resource Book 5

**with Online Resources**

British English

**Kate Cory-Wright with Caroline Nixon**
**& Michael Tomlinson**

**Cambridge University Press**
www.cambridge.org/elt

**Cambridge Assessment English**
www.cambridgeenglish.org

Information on this title: www.cambridge.org/9781316629475



First published 2009
Second edition 2015
Updated second edition 2017
Reprinted 2019

Printed in Great Britain by CPI Group (UK) Ltd, Croydon CRO 4YY

*A catalogue record for this publication is available from the British Library*

ISBN 978-1-316-629475 Teacher's Resource Book with Online Audio 5
ISBN 978-1-316-627709 Pupil's Book 5
ISBN 978-1-316-628782 Activity Book with Online Resources 5
ISBN 978-1-316-627945 Teacher's Book 5
ISBN 978-1-316-629000 Class Audio CDs 5 (3 CDs)
ISBN 978-1-316-628560 Language Portfolio 5
ISBN 978-1-316-629819 Interactive DVD with Teacher's Booklet 5 (PAL/NTSC)
ISBN 978-1-316-628041 Presentation Plus 5
ISBN 978-1-316-628713 Posters 5

Additional resources for this publication at www.cambridge.org/kidsbox



# Thanks and acknowledgements

**The authors would like to thank the following editors:**

Bridget Kelly, Lynne Rushton and Liane Grainger

Kate Cory-Wright would also like to thank Janine Berger: freelance teacher trainer and materials writer, Quito, Ecuador.

**The authors and publishers are grateful to the following illustrators:**

FLP; Graham Kennedy; Gwyneth Williamson; Jo Taylor; Ken Oliver c/o The Art Agency; Lisa Smith c/o Sylvie Poggio; Theresa Tibbetts c/o Beehive

**The authors and publishers are grateful to the following for permission to reproduce photographic material:**

© jeff giniewicz / istock: p.21, © Graham Pearce / Shutterstock: p.35, © Vladimir Sazonov / istock: p.61, © Christian Musat / istock: p.61.

**The publishers are grateful to the following contributors:**

Pentacorbig: concept design, cover design, book design and page make-up
Wild Apple Design: second edition cover design and page make-up
John Green and Tim Woolf, TEFL Audio: audio recordings
Songs written and produced by Robert Lee, Dib Dib Dub Studios
hyphen S.A.: editorial management

# Contents

**Introduction** 4

**Teacher's notes and worksheets**

Welcome to our ezine 8

Unit 1: Time for television 15

Unit 2: People at work 22

Unit 3: City life 29

Unit 4: Disaster! 36

Unit 5: Material things 43

Unit 6: Senses 50

Unit 7: Natural world 57

Unit 8: World of sport 64

Festivals 71

**Tests**

Test Units Welcome–2 76

Test Units 3–4 91

Test Units 5–6 106

Test Units 7–8 121

**Test key and audioscript** 136

# Introduction

- This Teacher's Resource Book is designed to help you and your pupils make the most of *Kid's Box 5* as well as provide practice for *Cambridge English: Young Learners* Tests. There are two main sections in this Book:
  - Worksheets
  - Practice tests

## Worksheets

- There are two Reinforcement worksheets and two Extension worksheets per unit. The former are designed for revision and to help those pupils who need extra practice, whilst the latter are designed to cater for the needs of fast finishers. These worksheets not only provide a resource for mixed-ability classes but also offer material to set as homework or for the rest of the class to use while you work individually with a pupil on a Speaking test.
- Reinforcement worksheet 1 for each unit focuses on key structures, whilst Reinforcement worksheet 2 revises vocabulary. Extension worksheet 1 is more challenging. It is designed for fast finishers who need a more cognitively demanding type of activity. Extension worksheet 2 is skills based. Reading, writing, listening and speaking are practised.
- There is also a Song worksheet for each unit. These always give the song lyrics and a song-based activity which varies from unit to unit. These worksheets are best done once pupils are familiar with the song. The songs are provided online on the *Kid's Box* website but you can also use the Class Audio CDs. Please note that the track numbers refer to *Kid's Box 5 Online Audio.*
- Finally, each unit has a content-based Topic worksheet. As explained in the Teacher's Book, the content-based lessons in the Pupil's Book and Activity Book aim to teach and reinforce understanding of subject topics which pupils learn in their other school classes, through the medium of English. Thus, there are dual aims: that of learning subject content and that of learning language. The Topic worksheets in this book add to the content-based pages in the Pupil's Book and Activity Book.
- There is a page of teaching notes before the worksheets for each unit. These notes include Optional follow-up activities, which add a useful extra dimension to each worksheet. You may find that one type of follow-up activity works better than another with your particular class, in which case you can use the suggestions as a springboard for adapting other worksheets.
- You may find, according to the particular interests of a pupil, that in one unit, he/she needs a Reinforcement worksheet whilst in other units, or at other times, the same pupil can more profitably do an Extension worksheet. Fast finishers may want/need to do Reinforcement and Extension worksheets.
- You can also use the worksheets as fillers or alternative activities when, for example, some other activity has interfered with the normal running of the class.
- The worksheets can also be used as models for you or your pupils to develop further practice activities. Creating exercises is an excellent way for pupils to consolidate their learning and they will enjoy swapping them with their friends.
- You may find it useful to keep a record of the worksheets each pupil has completed.
- After the resources for each unit, there are two worksheets for each of the following festivals:
  - Christmas
  - Easter
- There are teaching notes for the Festivals section.

## Practice tests

- There are four practice tests; the first covering the first three units of the Pupil's Book and the rest covering two units each. The tests are suitable for all classes, as they review the vocabulary and structures of the preceding units. In addition, they offer specific practice for the Flyers level of *Cambridge English: Young Learners* Tests. The focus here is on the various activity types and the test format.
- The more familiar the pupils are with these activity types, the more confidence they will have if they take Flyers, having completed *Kid's Box 6*.

## Flyers activity types in *Kid's Box 5* tests

| Task | Expected response | Tips |
|---|---|---|
| **Listening**<br>25 minutes | | **Ensure pupils know that each listening text is heard twice.** |
| Part 1<br>Listening for names and descriptions | Draw lines to match names to people in a picture. | Familiarise pupils with the names in the tests and ensure that they know which names are male and female and which can be both: e.g. *Alex, Kim, Pat* and *Sam*. Point out the example, where a line has been drawn from a name to a person in the picture. Pupils should listen to all the information about each person before making a decision. This information may be physical characteristics, clothes, actions or locations. There may be two people with blond hair but it will be other distinguishing features which identify exactly the person being spoken about. |

| Task | Expected response | Tips |
|---|---|---|
| Part 2<br>Listening for names, spellings and other information | Write words or numbers. | Encourage pupils to look at the picture and the title and to understand the situation in which the information is being given. Get them to read the prompts and try to imagine the kind of answer, e.g. a day of the week, a time, a name etc. Practise spelling out words for pupils to write down the letters correctly and saying large numbers up to 1001 and ordinals up to 31st. |
| Part 3<br>Listening for words, names and detailed information | Match pictures with illustrated words or names by writing a letter in the box. | Pupils should read carefully the introductory question at the top of the page to help them understand the general content and context of the questions. Pupils should be aware that the information in the left-hand column is not given in the same order as on the recording. There are eight options given, which the pupils have to match to the things in the left-hand column. They should be aware that, although all eight options are mentioned in the recording, only six of them are correct. They should not assume that the first word they hear is the correct one. |
| Part 4<br>Listening for specific information of various kinds | Tick the box under the correct picture. | Ensure that pupils listen to the whole of each part of the dialogue before deciding on their answer. All three picture options are mentioned but only one is correct. |
| Part 5<br>Listening for words, colours and specific information | Carry out instructions to colour and write. | Practise colour vocabulary (*black*, *blue*, *brown*, *green*, *grey*, *orange*, *pink*, *purple*, *red*, *yellow*) and ensure that pupils have the necessary coloured pencils for the test. There are two of each item in the picture. Train pupils to listen carefully for the exact description and/or location to decide which item they have to colour.<br>Remind pupils that, as well as colouring, they have to write words on the picture. |
| **Reading and Writing**<br>40 minutes | | **Correct spelling is required in all parts of the Reading and Writing Test.**<br>Encourage pupils to write clearly. It is often better not to use joined-up writing. Train pupils to write only as much as they need to. Give time limits when doing classroom tasks, to help pupils learn time management. |
| Part 1<br>Choosing the correct words to match given definitions | Copy correct words next to definitions. | Give pupils practice reading the whole sentence. There are often several possible options in the words around the text but only one which is completely correct. Discuss the different options with pupils and why only one of them is correct.<br>Give pupils practice in accurate copying. Remind pupils to copy the whole option and not to add anything extra.<br>Train pupils to check and correct their spelling. |
| Part 2<br>Reading and completing a conversation by choosing the best response | Choose the correct response by writing a letter. | Remind pupils to read all the options before choosing the correct one. Remind them to take extra care not just to choose an answer because it has the same word in it as the statement before it. Point out that there are two answers which they do not need.<br>Practise appropriate responses, not just to questions, but also to statements.<br>Give practice with the use of set expressions, e.g. *Fine, thanks.* / *So do I* and with short *yes/no* answers. |

| Task | Expected response | Tips |
|---|---|---|
| Part 3<br>Reading a story and choosing the best words to complete it | Choose and copy missing words correctly. Tick a box to choose the best title for the story. | Encourage pupils to read the whole text before trying to complete the first gap and then to read the text immediately surrounding the gap.<br>Give practice guessing which type of word (noun, adjective, singular, plural, verb etc.) could go into a gap and then in choosing an appropriate word from the box.<br>Give pupils practice reading stories and then giving a brief phrase to say what the gist of the story is. |
| Part 4<br>Reading and understanding a text and choosing grammatical words to complete it | Select the correct word from a choice of three options and copy it in the corresponding gap. | Encourage pupils to read the whole text before trying to complete the first gap and then to read the text immediately surrounding the gap. They should then choose an appropriate word from the list. Remind pupils to choose a word only from the three options given and to copy it exactly into the space. |
| Part 5<br>Reading a story and completing sentences about the story | Complete sentences about a story by writing 1, 2, 3 or 4 words. | Remind pupils that there can be 1, 2, 3 or 4 words missing from each gap but that they must not write more than four words. Train pupils to predict an outline of the story from the picture and the title. Give pupils practice in understanding what is being referred to in a text, especially the meaning of pronouns.<br>All words in every answer are taken from the text. Pupils should ensure that words chosen to complete sentences are copied correctly. |
| Part 6<br>Reading a short text and providing the missing words | Complete a text by writing words in the gaps. No answer options given. | Practise common collocations with pupils such as: *ask for, read about, take a photo*. Encourage them to read the whole text and guess what words are missing. Remind them that there is only one word missing from each gap. |
| Part 7<br>Writing a story from 3 picture prompts | Write 20 or more words. | Encourage pupils to describe scenes.<br>Review vocabulary in topic groups.<br>Practise linking sentences. |
| **Speaking**<br>7–9 minutes | | The Speaking tests are designed to test pupils' interactive listening ability, production of extended responses and pronunciation. They are required to follow simple instructions, talk about different pictures, and to answer simple questions about themselves. If you can, arrange to swap classes with another English teaching colleague, to give pupils the opportunity to work with someone that they may not know as well. Photocopy, colour and cut out the two 'Find the Differences' scenes, the two 'Find Information' cards and the 'Tell the Story' pictures. Mount them on card and laminate, if possible, for future use. Prepare Reinforcement or Extension worksheets for the rest of the class to do while you conduct the Speaking test with individual pupils.<br>Make sure that each pupil feels comfortable before you begin the test. See the Test key and audioscript (pp 136 to 144) for instructions on how to begin each part of the four Speaking tests in this book. |
| Part 1<br>Understanding statements about a picture and responding with what is different about a second picture | Identify six differences between pictures. | The following examples are based on Units Welcome–2 Speaking test.<br>Show the pupil both 'Find the Differences' cards. Say that some things are different between the two pictures and give an example e.g. *In my picture, the teacher is wearing trousers but in your picture the teacher is wearing a skirt.* Then give the pupil his/her copy. Say: *I'm going to say something about my picture. You tell me how your picture is different.* Then describe your picture, without pointing at it, to elicit responses from the pupil. Teacher: *In my picture, two girls are talking.* Pupil: *In my picture, two girls are reading a book.* If necessary, point at the relevant difference, repeat your statement and ask a back-up question: *What are the girls doing in your picture?*<br>Give pupils practice in class in describing differences between two similar pictures.<br>Ensure pupils can introduce themselves with their name, surname and age. |

| Task | Expected response | Tips |
| --- | --- | --- |
| Part 2<br>Answering questions with short responses and asking questions to find out information | Ask and respond to questions about two people or objects or situations. | Briefly show the pupil both 'Find Information' cards. Then give the pupil his/her copy. Introduce the subject and start to ask questions. The pupil should be able to answer the questions by looking at his/her card. Teacher: *This is Nick. I don't know anything about him but you do. So I'm going to ask you some questions. How old is Nick?* Pupil: *(He's) 13.* (T): *Does he think documentaries are interesting or boring?* (P): *Boring.* Help pupils by pointing at the relevant information if necessary. Complete the questions, then swap roles.<br>Give pupils practice in class in asking and answering questions with question words *Who, What, When, Where, How old, How many* etc. They should also be able to ask and answer questions with *or*, e.g. *Does he live in a house or a flat?* |
| Part 3<br>Understanding the beginning of a story and then continuing it based on a series of pictures | Describe each picture in turn. | Show the pupil the 'Tell the Story' card and give them time to look at it. Indicate the sequence by pointing. Introduce the story and describe the first picture: *These pictures tell a story. Just look at the pictures first. It's Tuesday. Michael is going to take a science test on Friday. He likes science and he wants to get a good mark. Now you go on telling the story.* Many variations in content and form are possible. If necessary, point at the pictures, and ask questions about them: *What time is it? What's Michael doing with his mum? Why? What's he going to do each day? What must/mustn't he do when he is studying?* Do not expect long sentences or highly developed storytelling skills. Pupils should only be able to say a few words about each picture.<br>Give pupils practice in class in telling picture stories. |
| Part 4<br>Understanding and responding to personal questions | Answer personal questions. | This part of the test is a chance for pupils to answer simple questions about themselves and their everyday lives that are related to the other parts of the test. The questions should cover a range of tenses that the pupils have already studied in class.<br>For example, introduce the subject by asking about the pupil's evenings and continue asking questions to elicit responses.<br>Teacher: *Now let's talk about your evenings. Are you going to watch television tonight?* Pupil: *Yes.*<br>(T): *What kind of TV programmes do you like?*<br>(P): *Cartoons.*<br>(T): *What time do you go to bed?*<br>(P): *(I go to bed) at nine o'clock.*<br>Give pupils practice in class in answering questions about themselves, their families and friends, their homes, their school and free time activities, their likes and dislikes. Make sure they know how to say: *Hello, Goodbye* and *Thank you* and *Sorry, I don't understand.* |

# Teacher's notes

## Reinforcement worksheet 1

- Pupils guess which school subjects Sophia, Frank, and Oliver like / don't like. Then they read the texts and fill in the gaps. Pupils read the speech bubbles and decide which character said each one. Finally, pupils complete the last three speech bubbles based on their own interests and favourite subjects.

**Key: 2)** 1 Sophia likes music. She doesn't like history. 2 Frank likes science. He doesn't like computer studies. 3 Oliver likes art. He doesn't like geography. **3)** Oliver, Sophia, Frank.

- ***Optional follow-up activity:*** On four separate strips of paper, each pupil writes four sentences: two about what subjects they like and two about subjects they don't like. Pupils should use *like / don't like + ing*. Working in groups, they jumble the papers in the middle of the table, then take turns to pick one up and read it out. The group has to guess who wrote it.

## Reinforcement worksheet 2

- Pupils look at the example words in the wordsearch: *geography* and *sport*. Point out that the words can go backwards and upwards, as well as forwards and down. Pupils find the school subjects. They then complete the sentences with the words, by reading the definitions.

**Key: 2)** 2 dictionary, 3 sport, 4 music, 5 geography, 6 art, 7 history, 8 maths, 9 exams, 10 French.

- ***Optional follow-up activity:*** Pupils work in groups miming subjects from the list for the others to guess.

## Extension worksheet 1

- Check before using this worksheet that pupils can cope with the maths and know the relevant symbols.

  Go through the example to establish that, in this case, a pattern is made by adding two each time. Pupils work out what they must add for the other questions and then complete the patterns.

  Pupils do the maths puzzles and write their answers in the crossword.

**Key: 1)** 1 eight, ten (increases by two each time), 2 twelve, fifteen (increases by three each time), 3 forty, fifty (increases by ten each time), 4 twenty-four, thirty (increases by six each time), 5 twenty-eight, thirty-five (increases by seven each time). **2)** 2 eleven, 3 fifteen, 4 twelve, 5 three, 6 twenty. The number across is **eleven**.

- ***Optional follow-up activity:*** Pupils write maths puzzles for their friends. Encourage them to use words rather than figures.

## Extension worksheet 2

F towards

- Remind pupils about the City School ezine. Pupils read the interview between the children and their head teacher and write in the correct questions from the list on the right. Then they listen to the interview to check their answers. They can practise the interview in groups of four.

**Key:** 2 Mr Kelly: How can I help you? 3 Shari: How old is City School? 4 Dan: How many students are there? 5 Shari: When do children start school? 6 Dan: And when do children leave this school?

- ***Optional follow-up activity:*** Pupils prepare questions for a teacher at their school. Practise the questions with them. If possible, ask them to carry out their interview with a real teacher (or role-play the interview in class with other pupils).

## Song worksheet

- Pupils listen to the song and tick subjects that the singers like.

  Point out some words in the first verse of the song with different numbers of syllables (e.g. *study*=2, *afternoon*=3). Ask pupils to clap the number of syllables. Then pupils circle the words as instructed in each verse. Now the class can sing the song.

**Key: 1)** Pictures ticked should be: geography, history, science, sport, languages. **2)** 1 because/Friday/study/morning, 2 I/and/to/too/my/in/the, 3 computer, 4 languages, Japanese, dictionary.

- ***Optional follow-up activity:*** Pupils play Hangman in class, using school subjects. When a pupil guesses the word, he/she says how many syllables the word has.

## Topic worksheet

- Help pupils pronounce the word *archaeologist* (*ar-kee-**ol**-o-gist*). Using the illustrations pre-teach: *skeleton, to dig, local, skull, tomb, cave* and *gold*. Pupils read the text and label the remaining illustrations. Pupils then read the text again and correct the sentences.

**Key: 1)** staircase, King Tutankhamun, jewellery, archaeologist. **2)** 2 Archaeologists often find paintings in caves. 3 Teeth can tell archaeologists how old the person was and what they ate. 4 The Incas lived in Machu Picchu more than five hundred years ago. 5 Howard Carter found King Tutankhamun after digging for six years / for a long time. 6 King Tutankhamun was found inside a big room / a tomb (behind a staircase and a wall).

- ***Optional follow-up activity:*** Pupils discuss and then write about the question: *Would you like to be an archaeologist? Why? / Why not?*

# Reinforcement worksheet 1

**1** **Look at the pictures of Sophia, Frank and Oliver. Guess their favourite school subjects. What subjects do you think they don't like?**

Sophia

Frank

Oliver

**2** **Now read about them and complete the sentences. Were you right?**

| Sophia | Frank | Oliver |
|---|---|---|
| I like singing and playing the guitar. I don't like learning about the past. | I like to learn about plants and the human body. I don't like the internet. | I like taking photos and drawing. I don't like learning about other countries. |

1 Sophia likes music ............................ . She doesn't like ............................ .

2 Frank likes ............................ . He doesn't like ............................ .

3 Oliver likes ............................ . He doesn't like ............................ .

**3** **Who would like to put these things in the ezine? Write Sophia, Frank or Oliver under the sentences.**

I'd like to put a painting in the ezine.

............................

I'd like to write about my favourite singer and her new CD.

............................

I'd like to write about animals and what they eat.

............................

**4** **Write three things that you would like to put in an ezine.**

I'd like to put ............................ in the ezine.

I'd like to write about ............................ .

............................

  

Welcome!

# Reinforcement worksheet 2

## 1 Find and circle ten school subjects.

| | | | | | | | | |
|---|---|---|---|---|---|---|---|---|
| g | e | o | g | r | a | p | h | y |
| n | h | h | c | n | e | r | f | r |
| v | s | i | h | o | x | j | i | a |
| m | i | s | g | p | a | l | o | n |
| a | t | t | e | r | m | t | i | o |
| t | r | o | p | s | s | m | c | i |
| h | e | r | t | e | r | a | r | t |
| s | g | y | h | a | r | m | i | c |
| e | m | u | s | i | c | s | a | i |
| t | s | c | i | e | n | c | e | d |

~~geography~~
~~sport~~
history
art
exams
dictionary
French
maths
music
science

## 2 Complete the sentences using the school subjects.

1 I like ......science...... . We study animals, plants and the human body in this subject.

2 I use a .................... to help me understand new words.

3 Zee loves playing football and basketball. His favourite subject is .................... .

4 David likes .................... . He's good at singing, playing the guitar and the piano.

5 We learn about different countries in .................... .

6 Sarah loves drawing and taking photographs. Her favourite subject is .................... .

7 In .................... we can learn about the past.

8 Try this! 10 + 20 – 3 / 9 = 3. .................... is easy!

9 We have to study a lot before we take .................... .

10 If you speak .................... , you can talk to people in France.

Welcome!

# Extension worksheet 1

## 1 Complete the number patterns. Write the numbers.

1

| | | | | |
|---|---|---|---|---|
| two | four | six | eight | ten |

2

| | | | | |
|---|---|---|---|---|
| three | six | nine | | |

3

| | | | | |
|---|---|---|---|---|
| ten | twenty | thirty | | |

4

| | | | | |
|---|---|---|---|---|
| six | twelve | eighteen | | |

5

| | | | | |
|---|---|---|---|---|
| seven | fourteen | twenty-one | | |

## 2 Complete the maths puzzles. Write your answers in the crossword. What's the number in the black boxes?

1 8 + 8 – 6 = ......10......

2 9 x 2 – 7 = ..............

3 2 x 5 + 35 / 3 = ..............

4 4 x 6 / 2 = ..............

5 5 x 7 + 10 / 15 = ..............

6 6 x 5 – 20 + 10 = ..............

The number in the black boxes is:

................................ .

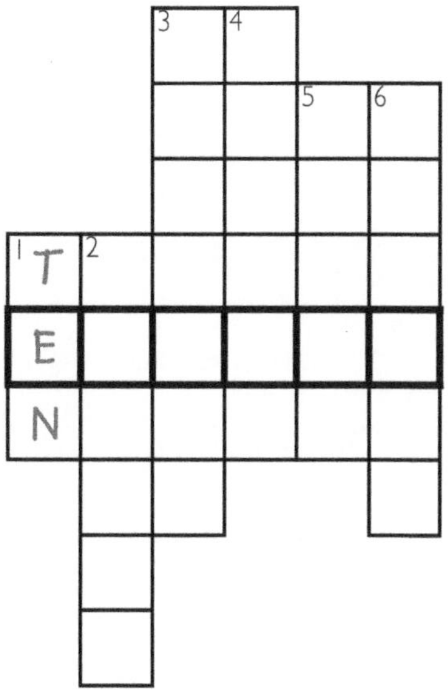


  

Welcome!

# Extension worksheet 2

**1** **For their ezine, Alvin, Shari and Dan are interviewing Mr Kelly, the head teacher of City School.**

**Read the questions and complete the interview.**

**Alvin:** Good afternoon, Mr Kelly.

1 How are you?

**Mr Kelly:** I'm fine, thank you.

2 ______

**Shari:** We'd like to ask you some questions for our ezine.

3 ______

**Mr Kelly:** It's fifty-seven years old.

**Dan:** 4 ______

**Mr Kelly:** There are five hundred and eighty-three students.

**Shari:** 5 ______

**Mr Kelly:** Children start school when they are four years old.

**Dan:** 6 ______

**Mr Kelly:** When they're twelve.

**Alvin:** OK, that's all. Thank you!

**Mr Kelly:** You're welcome. Good luck with your ezine!

How old is City School?

When do children start school?

~~How are you?~~

How many students are there?

And when do children leave this school?

How can I help you?

**2** 2 **Listen and check.**

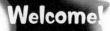

# Song worksheet

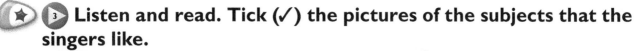

**1 Listen and read. Tick (✓) the pictures of the subjects that the singers like.**

☑

☐

☐

☐

☐

☐

☐

Because school is cool, it's where we go.
From Monday to Friday, I'm sure you know.
We study and we play, that's what we do.
We do it in the morning and the afternoon!

I really love geography,
And I enjoy history.
I like to study science too!
My favourite subject in the afternoon.

Before lunch we have music,
And then computer studies,
And on Wednesday we do sport.
That's a class which is too short!

And I like to do languages,
Spanish, French and Japanese.
Lots of words in the dictionary,
For me to study and to read.

**2**

1 'Monday' has two syllables. Circle another two-syllable word in this verse.

2 Two one-syllable words are circled in this verse. Can you circle another one?

3 There is one three-syllable word in this verse. Can you circle it?

4 There are three three-syllable words in this verse. Can you circle them?

# Topic worksheet

## 1 Read about archaeologists. Label the pictures.

a cave

Archaeologists are interested in history. They often travel to countries where people lived thousands of years ago. They look at paintings in caves and find bones. They find things that people used every day.

When archaeologists find a skeleton, they ask many questions; for example, *How big is it? Is it a man, woman or child? Why is it there?* Sometimes they find the person's skull. Teeth can tell us how old the person was and what they ate.

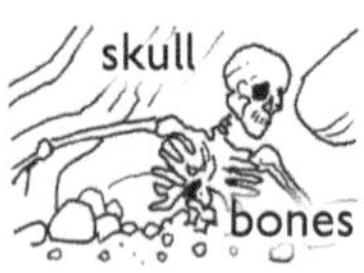


skeleton

Sometimes there are more questions than answers. Hiram Bingham went to Peru in South America. Local people told him about a 'city' on a mountain. Bingham found 'Machu Picchu'. He learned a lot about the Incas who lived there more than five hundred years ago. But there are still many questions. *Why did the Incas live there? Why did they leave? Why were most of the skeletons women?*

to dig

A famous archaeologist called Howard Carter dug in the sand in Egypt for six years. In 1922, he found a staircase and a wall. Behind these there was a big room. It was the tomb of King Tutankhamun. He was surrounded by jewellery and gold.

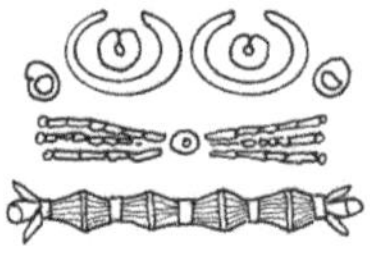

Archaeologists work in the sun, the rain and the cold. They look for answers for many years. Sometimes they never find them.

## 2 Correct the sentences.

1 Archaeologists are interested in maths.

Archaeologists are interested in history.

2 Archaeologists often find paintings in houses.

..............................................................

3 Teeth can tell archaeologists the colour of someone's hair.

..............................................................

4 The Incas live in Machu Picchu today.

..............................................................

5 Howard Carter found King Tutankhamun after digging for a short time.

..............................................................

6 King Tutankhamun was found on a mountain.

..............................................................

# 1 Teacher's notes

## Reinforcement worksheet 1

- Pupils compare the timetables and write five more differences.

**Key:** 2 Crazy Cat / Cool Cat at 1:45, 3 School Friends Episode 5/3 at 2:15, 4 Golf/Football at 2:45, 5 The Rosetta Stone at 3:00/3:15, 6 Quiz / The Weather at 3:50.

- ***Optional follow-up activity:*** Pupils write a plan of their favourite TV schedule (real or imaginary). Display these in the classroom, and ask pupils to vote for their favourite.

## Reinforcement worksheet 2

- Use the example to show pupils how to complete the missing word in each sentence, using the words on the TV, and then cross out each word as they use it. The aim is to cross four words in a straight line. The line can be horizontal or vertical, but not diagonal. Then use the first letter of these four words to complete Shari's sentence.

**Key: 1)** 2 channels, 3 quiz, 4 sports, 5 animals, 6 series, 7 boring, 8 weather, 9 turn on, 10 episodes. **2)** All the words in the last line on the right (***b**oring, **e**pisodes, **s**eries, **t**urn on*) are crossed out. Shari is saying: *Programmes about dinosaurs are the best!*

- ***Optional follow-up activity:*** Pupils invent definitions for the remaining six words: *cameraman, screen, action film, music video, funny, cartoon*.

## Extension worksheet 1

- Using a torch and a ball, explain that when the sun is in one half of the world, it's dark in the other half. Check pupils know the names of the cities and what countries they're in. Pupils then draw lines from the names to the dots on the map. Refer to an atlas if necessary. Then look at the map together, pointing out the different times in different places.

  Pupils write the time for each city using 'in the morning/ afternoon/at night'. To help pupils with the number of hours' difference between the cities, look at the clocks and ask questions, e.g. *It's 11:15 in London. What time is it in Paris?* (12:15) *So how many hours ahead is Paris?* (1 hour) *If it's 8:00 in London, what time is it in Paris?* (9:00).

| NY | **London** | Paris | Tokyo | Sydney |
|---|---|---|---|---|
| – 5 | **0** | + 1 | + 9 | + 11 |

  Choose different cities. Now pupils complete exercise 2.

**Key: 2)** 2 London: It's quarter past eleven in the morning. 3 Paris: It's quarter past twelve in the afternoon. 4 Tokyo: It's quarter past eight at night. 5 Sydney: It's quarter past ten at night. **3)** 1 It's quarter past four in Paris. 2 It's ten past eight in London. 3 It's quarter to eleven in Sydney. 4 It's Thursday in London!

- ***Optional follow-up activity:*** Play Pelmanism. Give each student four equally-sized pieces of card. On two of the cards they draw a clock face with a time on it. On the other two they write the corresponding time for each clock in words. Check that the faces and times match for each pair of cards. Working in groups of four, pupils place their 'clock' cards face down on one side of the table and the 'words' cards face down on the other. The first pupil picks up a 'clock face' card and says the time. If he/she is wrong, the card is replaced and the next pupil has a turn. If he/she is correct, he/she can pick up a 'words' card. If the two cards match, he/she keeps them. If not, he/she returns them to the table and the next pupil has a turn. The pupil with the most pairs of cards at the end is the winner.

## Extension worksheet 2

- Pupils read the TV Guide and write a word from the box for each channel. Then pupils read the guide a second time to help them circle the right answers to the questions.

**Key: 1)** Channel 2 – comedy, Channel 3 – series, Channel 4 – cartoon, Channel 5 – quiz. **2)** 2 a, 3 c, 4 b, 5 a.

- ***Optional follow-up activity:*** Pupils discuss which programmes from the TV guide they would like to watch and why.

## Song worksheet

- Pupils listen to and read the song and underline all the programme words. Then they draw happy and sad faces in the circles next to the programmes that the singer does/doesn't like. If necessary, help them with phrases like: *They're not for me / They're not my thing.*

**Key:** Happy faces – documentary, cartoon, sport, action films. Sad faces – TV, the news and weather, TV.

- ***Optional follow-up activity:*** Pupils personalise the song by replacing the underlined words with other programmes.

## Topic worksheet

- Pupils discuss a TV series that they know and like and who is involved in making it. Pupils read the text and match the jobs with the roles. Check their answers and help with any pronunciation difficulties.

**Key: 2)** 2 h, 3 b, 4 c, 5 e, 6 g, 7 f, 8 a.

- ***Optional follow-up activity:*** Revise superlatives (e.g. *the biggest, the most beautiful*). Then ask pupils to discuss which film-making job is the most interesting/important/ difficult/fun. Pupils discuss which one they would like to do and why.

Unit 1

# Reinforcement worksheet 1

**Find six differences between Channel TV1 and TV2. Write your answers.**

| CHANNEL TV1 | |
|---|---|
| 1:00 | The News |
| 1:45 | Crazy Cat cartoons |
| 2:15 | School Friends *Episode 5* |
| 2:45 | Golf |
| 3:00 | The Rosetta Stone |
| 3:50 | What do you know? (quiz) |

| CHANNEL TV2 | |
|---|---|
| 1:30 | The News |
| 1:45 | Cool Cat cartoons |
| 2:15 | School Friends *Episode 3* |
| 2:45 | Football |
| 3:15 | The Rosetta Stone |
| 3:50 | The Weather |

1 On TV1 the news is on at one o'clock. On TV2 the news is on at half past one.

2 On TV1 Crazy Cat cartoons is on at quarter to two. On TV2 ................ is on at ................

3 ................

4 ................

5 ................

6 ................

Unit 1

# Reinforcement worksheet 2

## 1 Complete the sentences and cross out the words on the TV.

1 The news................ tells us what is happening in the world.

2 TV1 and TV2 are the names of two c.......................... .

3 A TV competition where people answer questions is called a q.......................... .

4 We can watch football on a s.......................... programme.

5 Many cartoon characters are not people. They are a.......................... .

6 A story that you watch each week is called a s.......................... .

7 Some documentaries are not b.......................... . They are interesting.

8 This programme tells us if it is raining or snowing. It is called the w.......................... .

9 You have to t.............. .......... the TV when you want to watch it.

10 The parts of a series that you watch each week are called e.......................... .

| | | | |
|---|---|---|---|
| channels | cameraman | screen | boring |
| quiz | action film | sports | episodes |
| music video | weather | animals | series |
| funny | ~~news~~ | cartoon | turn on |

## 2 Which four crossed out words form a line? Use the first letters to complete what Shari is saying.

Programmes about dinosaurs are the .......................... !

Unit 1

# Extension worksheet 1

## 1 Draw lines to each city.

New York, USA London, UK Paris, France Tokyo, Japan Sydney, Australia

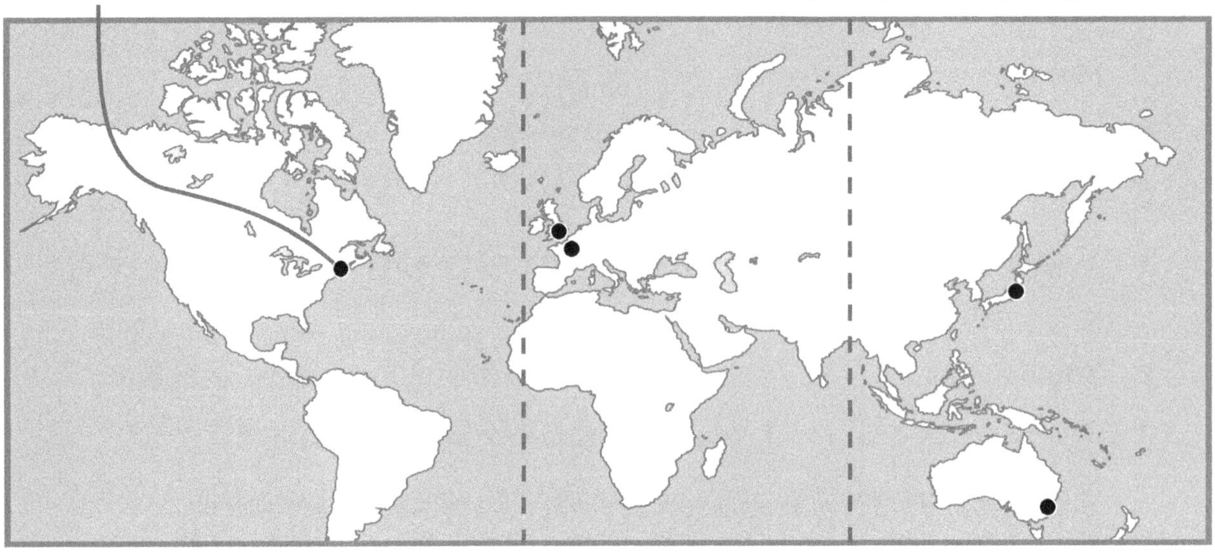

→ MORNING →← AFTERNOON →← NIGHT →

## 2 Write the time in each city.

1 New York: It's quarter past six in the morning.

2 London: ..........

3 Paris: ..........

4 Tokyo: ..........

5 Sydney: ..........

## 3 What time is it in these cities? Write your answers.

1 It's quarter past three in London. What time is it in Paris?

It's quarter past four in Paris.

2 It's ten past three in New York. What time is it in London?

It's ten past ..........

3 It's quarter to nine in Tokyo. What time is it in Sydney?

It's ..........

4 It's twenty past seven on Friday morning in Sydney. What day is it in London?

..........

Unit 1

# Extension worksheet 2

## 1 Read the TV Guide and choose words from the box for each channel.

| | | | |
|---|---|---|---|
| series | cartoon | ~~documentary~~ | the weather |
| quiz | music video | comedy | |

### Children's TV Guide

| Channel 1 | Channel 2 | Channel 3 | Channel 4 | Channel 5 |
|---|---|---|---|---|
| 4:00–5:00<br>Dolphin and whale special | 4:00–4:30<br>Clowntime | 4:00–4:45<br>Happy street | 4:00–5:40<br>Supermum 2 | 4:00–4:15<br>What do you know? |
| Do you know that dolphins never sleep? In today's programme we learn all about these amazing animals: where they live, what they eat and how clever they are. | Millie and Maisie the clowns are so funny! Why are they throwing paint and water? Why are they jumping up and down with eggs on their heads? Watch today's programme to find the answers. | Last week Sam and Jane found an old map in the school library. Where did it come from? Where can it take them? This week's episode answers these questions and lots more! | Now that Supermum's children are older, she's helping people with their animals! Have you lost your dog? Supermum can fly over the city and find it. She's fast and she's strong. The drawings in this film are great! | This programme is so exciting that you want it to be longer! Six people answer very difficult questions. The winner gets a holiday in Egypt. |
| documentary | ................ | ................ | ................ | ................ |

## 2 Read again and choose the right answer.

1 How long is *Supermum 2*?

**a)** half an hour **b)** an hour and a quarter **c)** an hour and forty minutes (circled)

2 What time does *Happy Street* finish?

**a)** at quarter to five **b)** at quarter past five **c)** at quarter to four

3 Which of these things don't the clowns use?

**a)**  **b)**  **c)** 

4 Dolphins are: **a)** not clever **b)** always awake **c)** very big birds

5 In *What do you know?* the winner gets:

**a)**  **b)** 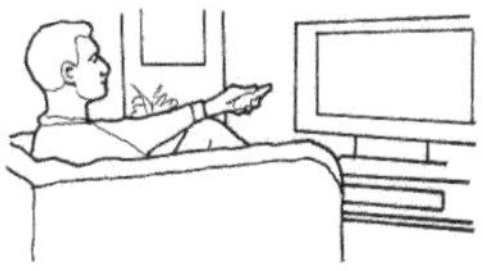 **c)** 

Unit 1

# Song worksheet

**4 Listen and read. Underline the TV programmes. Does the singer like these TV programmes? Draw a happy or sad face in the circles.**

I don't like TV, I don't like it much,

But there are some programmes that I sometimes watch.

On channel 1 at ten past three,

There's a really good documentary

About animals and where they live,

What they do and what they eat,

And on channel four at five to two,

They put on a great cartoon.

At one o'clock and then at seven,

They show the news and then the weather.

They're not my thing, they're not for me,

But I like the sport at half past three.

But what I like, what I love the best,

Are the action films, more than the rest.

They're on at quarter past four,

And at ten past seven, but I want more.

I don't like TV, I don't like it much,

But there are some programmes that I sometimes watch.

Unit 1

# Topic worksheet

## 1 What's your favourite TV series? Do you know how it's made?

A TV series is a story which we watch in many parts (or *episodes*). Sometimes we can watch one, two or more episodes in one week. Usually a TV series starts with an idea. If a producer likes the idea, he/she talks to a screenwriter, who writes the story. Then the producer speaks to a director, who has to decide where to film the series and what happens in each scene. Next the producer has to find money to pay for the series. After the film is made, the editors cut the film and join it together. Then the producer has to sell the series to TV channels around the world. And then we watch it!

### Who else makes the TV series?

You can often see a list of people who made the series at the end of a TV programme: the casting director, actors, camera crew and designers. Who are these people and what do they do?

Every series needs a good technical team, for example, a camera crew (the people who film the series). The TV series also needs people to manage the sound, lighting and special effects. Lots of artists and designers also help to make the series. They have to prepare the make-up and clothes for the actors, or design the set.

Of course, a good TV series needs good actors! They play the people in the series. The casting director has to choose the actors. Famous actors are expensive, so the casting director can't always choose famous people for the series!

## 2 Match the person with the job.

| | | | |
|---|---|---|---|
| 1 | The editor | a | films the series. |
| 2 | The screenwriter | b | finds the money for the series. |
| 3 | The producer | c | chooses the actors. |
| 4 | The casting director | d | cuts the film and joins it together. |
| 5 | The director | e | decides what happens in each scene. |
| 6 | Actors | f | prepare the make-up and clothes. |
| 7 | Designers | g | play the people in the series. |
| 8 | The camera crew | h | writes the story. |

# 2 Teacher's notes

## Reinforcement worksheet 1

- Look at the advertisement. If necessary pre-teach: *talent competition, to tell jokes, to joke*. Pupils read the dialogue and fill in the gaps, using the appropriate form of *going to*. Then pupils label the characters. After checking the answers, ask comprehension questions, e.g. *Is Peter really going to eat hamburgers?* (no), *What is Peter going to do?* (tell jokes).

**Key: 1)** 2 What are your friends going to do? 3 Mary's / Mary is going to dance. 4 What's / What is he going to do? 5 He's / He is going to play the guitar. 6 I'm / I am going to eat. 7 What are you going to eat? 8 You're / You are not going to eat hamburgers! 9 I'm / I am not going to do that! 10 What are you really going to do? 11 I'm / I am going to tell jokes. **2)** Peter, Mary.

- ***Optional follow-up activity:*** In groups of three, pupils act out the dialogue. Remind 'Peter' to be a bit naughty, 'Mum' and 'Dad' to be shocked.

## Reinforcement worksheet 2

- Pupils unscramble the words. Then they label each picture.

**Key:** 1 fire fighter, 2 dentist, 3 mechanic, 4 designer, 5 actor, 6 manager, 7 nurse, 8 pilot, 9 cook, 10 artist, 11 scientist, 12 journalist.

- ***Optional follow-up activity:*** Pupils write scrambled words for others to guess from one of the following themes: school subjects, types of TV programme, days of the week.

## Extension worksheet 1

- Practise asking and answering *yes/no* questions by giving a confident pupil a job title e.g. *dentist* and getting the class to ask him/her questions to guess what it is. He/She can only answer *yes* or *no*. Pre-teach *uniform* and *office*. Pupils read the interviews and work out which job each child is going to do.

**Key:** 2 basketball player, 3 mechanic, 4 pilot, 5 cook.

- ***Optional follow-up activity:*** Pupils interview each other in the same way, with *yes/no* questions to find out which job their partner has chosen.

## Extension worksheet 2

- Pupils look at the picture and discuss the questions. Listen to pupils' thoughts. Pupils listen to the recording and complete the table. You may want to go through each character one by one, playing the recording several times.

**Key (audioscript): John:** I usually work *at the weekends* because that's when people have parties. I go to *people's houses* and wear a red nose. I use balls and do things to make people laugh. I love my job because *it's happy and it's fun!* (He's a clown.)

**Robert:** I work *from Monday to Friday* in *an office*. I make telephone calls and use a computer to type important letters and emails. I tell people what to do. I like this job because *I love working with people and I'm never tired!* (He's a manager.)

**Emma:** I go to work *every night*. I work *in a busy hospital*. I'm not a doctor but I help people who are ill or injured. I'm often tired but *my job is always interesting*. That's why I love it! (She's a nurse.)

**Jane:** I do my job *from half past seven in the morning to five in the afternoon*. I have to get up very early so that I can get to *school* before my pupils arrive. I work very hard teaching children to speak French. *It's really good to work with children*. I don't want to do anything else! (She's a French teacher.)

- ***Optional follow-up activity:*** Pupils imagine they do one of these jobs and write about their normal day at work for an ezine.

## Song worksheet

- Pupils listen to the song and fill in the gaps. They then draw a picture in each box to represent an action for each verse.

**Key:** work, best, sleep x4, show, good, help, in x4, job, day, best, sleep, job, work, sleep.

- ***Optional follow-up activity:*** Ask the whole class to choose a job and make up a verse about it together. Pupils then choose a job for themselves and write their own verse. They can try to make it rhyme if they feel confident enough. The new verses could be written on the board and then sung by the class.

## Topic worksheet

- Pre-teach: *earn* and *factories*. Pupils read the text and answer the questions. Finally, pupils draw a picture of a present they would like to give to a poor child, and write a short description of the present and why they want to give it.

**Key: 1)** 1 They grow food in fields//on farms, they sell sweets, they clean shoes, they make shoes and clothes in factories, they ask people for money in the streets. 2 Answers might include: beds, food, toys, time (to play), lessons, shoes, clothes and sweets.

- ***Optional follow-up activity:*** Write the following question and answers on the board and check that pupils understand them. Then put pupils into groups and ask them to rank the answers according to their importance and discuss. Question: *Why is education important?* Answers: *to learn to read and write, to find a good job, to meet friends, to know about the world, to have time to play and do sport, to learn languages, to learn about computers.*

Unit 2

# Reinforcement worksheet 1

**1 Peter is talking to his mum and dad about the School Talent Competition. Complete what they say with *am/is/are going to.***

SCHOOL TALENT COMPETITION

Can you dance? Can you act? Are you good at singing or playing the guitar? Come to the Talent Competition! There are going to be lots of prizes!

See you on Friday 24th at 8pm!

**Mum:** What (1) ....are.... you ....going to.... do in the School Talent Competition?

**Peter:** I don't know, Mum.

**Dad:** Well, what (2) ................ your friends ................ do?

**Peter:** Mary (3) ................................ dance. But I hate dancing.

**Mum:** What about John? What (4) ................ he ................................ do?

**Peter:** He (5) ................................ play the guitar.

**Dad:** You're good at playing the guitar, Peter. Why don't you do that?

**Peter:** No, I don't like playing the guitar. Wait! I've got a good idea.
I (6) ................................ eat!

**Mum:** Eat? What (7) ................ you ................................ eat?

**Peter:** Five hamburgers in two minutes!

**Dad:** Oh Peter! You (8) ................ not ................................ eat hamburgers!

**Mum:** No Peter. That's not a very good idea!

**Peter:** I'm joking. Of course I (9) ................ not ................ do that!

**Mum:** What (10) ................ you really ................................ do?

**Peter:** I (11) ................................ tell jokes. I'm good at telling jokes!

**2 Write the names under the pictures.**

............John............

................................

................................

Unit 2

# Reinforcement worksheet 2

## Find the words and label the pictures.

| | | | |
|---|---|---|---|
| eruns | nurse | sntedit | d.................... |
| edsiengr | d.................... | torca | a.................... |
| steincsit | s.................... | isanljourt | j.................... |
| chemanci | m.................... | iltop | p.................... |
| eieffigrhtr | f.................... | okoc | c.................... |
| mnaarge | m.................... | ttiasr | a.................... |

1 ....................

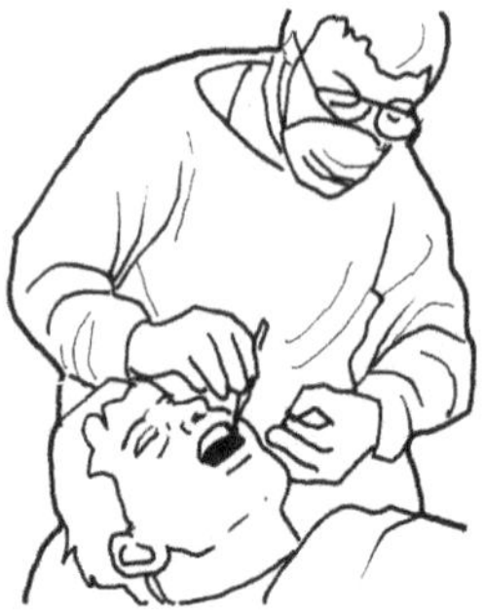
2 ....................

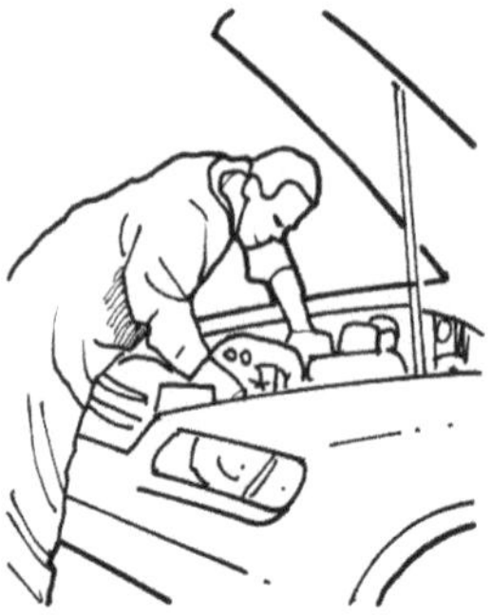
3 ....................

4 ....................

5 ....................

6 ....................

7 nurse

8 ....................

9 ....................

10 ....................

11 ....................

12 ....................

# Unit 2 Extension worksheet 1

**Pupils from City School are asking each other questions about what job they are going to do. They can only answer *yes* or *no*! Read their interviews and find the job.**

| | | | |
|---|---|---|---|
| painter | basketball player | pilot | footballer |
| manager | mechanic | ~~writer~~ | cook |

**1**

Are you going to work with other people?
In this job, are you going to use a laptop?
Are you going to work in an office?
Are you going to work at home?
Are you going to be a writer ?

No.
Yes.
No.
Yes.
Yes!

**2**

Are you going to work in the same place every day?
Are you going to do sport?
Are you going to use your feet to move a ball?
Are you going to be a ................................ ?

No.
Yes.
No.
Yes!

**3**

Are you going to work in the same place every day?
Are you going to use a laptop?
Are you going to use your hands?
Are you going to work with cars?
Are you going to be a ................................ ?

Yes.
No.
Yes.
Yes.
Yes!

**4**

Are you going to work in the same place every day?
Are you going to go to lots of different countries?
Are you going to wear a special uniform?
Is doing sport important for this job?
Are you going to be a ................................ ?

No.
Yes.
Yes.
No.
Yes!

**5**

Are you going to work with other people?
Are you going to use a laptop in this job?
Are you going to make something?
Are you going to make something that people need every day?
Are you going to be a ................................ ?

Yes.
No.
Yes.
Yes.
Yes!

Unit 2

# Extension worksheet 2

**1** **Look at the picture. What does this man do? When and where does he work? Does he enjoy his job?**

**2** **5** **Listen to the people talk about their jobs. Complete the table. What do you think each person does?**

| Name | When do they work? | Where do they work? | Why do they like their job? | What do you think they do? |
|---|---|---|---|---|
| John | at the weekends | | | |
| Robert | | | | |
| Emma | | | | |
| Jane | | | | |

Unit 2

# Song worksheet

6 **Listen and complete the song. Draw something that happens in each verse.**

He's going to do the job,
He's going to ......work...... all day.
He's going to do his ............,
Then ............ and play,
............ and play,
............ and play,
............ and play.

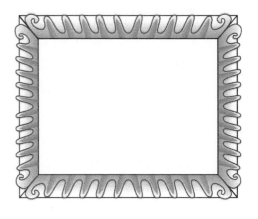

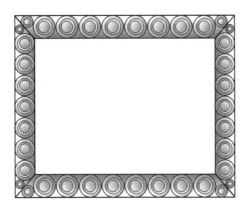

She's going to ............ the kids,
She's going to teach ............ rules.
She's going to ............ them all,
And work ............ schools,
Work ............ schools,
Work ............ schools,
Work ............ schools.

They're going to do the ............,
They're going to work all ............,
They're going to do their ............,
Then ............ and play.
They're going to do the ............,
Then ............ all day.
Then ............ and play.

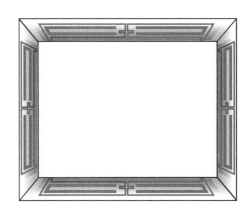

Unit 2

# Topic worksheet

## 1 Read about children who don't go to school and answer the questions.

Are there some days when you don't want to go to school? Many children around the world don't go to school. But they don't stay at home either. These children have to work.

Some children work in the fields or on farms. They help to grow food for their families to eat. Some children work in the cities selling sweets or cleaning shoes to get money for their families. Some children make shoes or clothes in factories. And some children walk along the streets asking people for money.

Life is hard for these children. They work because they are very poor. Sometimes they don't have food. Sometimes they don't have a bed to sleep in. These children don't have toys to play with, and they don't have time to play. If they go to school, they can't earn money and if they don't earn money, they can't buy food to eat.

So next time you don't want to go to school, think of the millions of children who can't go to school.

1 What kinds of work do poor children do? Find examples in the text.

a *They grow food in the fields.* b ..........

c .......... d ..........

2 Find four things in the text that money can buy for us.

.......... .......... .......... ..........

## 2 You are going to give a working child a present. Draw a picture of your present and write a note to him or her.

*I would like to give you this because*

..........

..........

..........

..........

# 3 Teacher's notes

## Reinforcement worksheet 1

- Ask pupils to look at the map. Point out key places, like the river and the streets. Tell them that they are in *The High Street*, near the *bus stop*. Using the map, pupils read each dialogue and circle the correct word.

**Key:** 2 past, 3 right, 4 first, 5 third.

- ***Optional follow-up activity:*** Pupils practise giving directions to different places. They can use the map or the classroom. To turn your classroom into a 'map', move tables and chairs to make 'streets'. Label some chairs with key places, e.g. *park, zoo*. A pupil stands at the board and asks for directions. Pupils tell him/her how to get to the place. The pupil 'walks the route' around the classroom.

## Reinforcement worksheet 2

- Pupils unscramble the letters to make words for things in the town, then put the correct word under each picture. Then they complete the clues to find the treasure.

**Key: 1)** (from left to right) supermarket, hospital, bank, train station, bus stop, taxi, post office, theatre, university, museum, castle, hotel, stadium, police station, restaurant, airport. **2)** 1 s<u>c</u>hool, 2 b<u>a</u>nk, 3 po<u>s</u>t office, 4 <u>t</u>heatre, 5 hote<u>l</u>, 6 mus<u>e</u>um. The treasure is in the **castle**.

- ***Optional follow-up activity:*** Pupils write clues for each other like the ones in exercise 2, to guess different places in the town. Confident pupils could try to make their own 'treasure hunt' as in the worksheet.

## Extension worksheet 1

- Pupils complete the sentences 1 to 8 with the superlative. Then pupils read sentences a–h and match them to 1 to 8.

**Key: 1)** 3 largest, 4 smallest, 5 fastest, 6 most beautiful, 7 most interesting, 8 oldest. **2)** b 1, c 4, d 3, e 7, f 2, g 6, h 5.

- ***Optional follow-up activity:*** Pupils imagine the ugliest/biggest/smallest or most beautiful building in the world and write about it. They can draw a picture too and present this to each other in small groups.

## Extension worksheet 2

- Pupils listen to the children's directions and use colours to draw their routes home from school. Then pupils write directions to Katy's house.

**Key: 1) (audioscript): Sally** (example black line): I leave school, turn left and go along Blue Street. I cross The High Street and Low Road and go straight on. I live opposite the fire station in the second house on the left.
**Ben** (blue line): I go along Blue Street and turn left into The High Street. Then I turn right into Green Street. I live in a big building on the left.
**Helen** (red line): I go along Blue Street and turn left into The High Street. I take the second street on the right. It's called Red Street. I live on the corner of Red Street and Low Road, opposite the cinema.
**Fred** (green line): I walk along Blue Street and cross The High Street. I turn left into Low Road and then right at Green Street. I live opposite the supermarket in the third house on the left.
**Jim** (brown line): I walk along Blue Street and turn left at The High Street. Then I take the first left and walk to the end of Green Street. I live in a boat on the River Eight.
**2)** Walk along Blue Street and turn left into The High Street. Then take the first right at Green Street. I live next to the Book shop. (Other routes are possible.)

- ***Optional follow-up activity:*** Pupils write directions from their school to their homes. If they live too far away, they can give directions to places nearer the school.

## Song worksheet

- Pupils match the rhyming words and add them to the words of the song. Play the song to check their answers. Ask pupils to skim read the song, looking for places (e.g. *theatre*) and tick the pictures of places in the list that the singer visited to find the five places he didn't visit. Now they sing the song.

**Key: 1)** 2 d, 3 a, 4 e, 5 b. **2)** See Pupil's Book, page 31. **4)** He *didn't* visit the toy shop, bank, swimming pool, library.

- ***Optional follow-up activity:*** Draw two columns on the board. Label them *street/eat* and *late/eight*. Point out the different spelling of similar sounds. In small groups pupils think of more words that rhyme with *street/eat* and *late/eight*. They write them on the board. They earn points for each correct word. (Ideas: *street/eat – feet, meat, seat, cheat, meet*; *late/eight – date, plate, ate.*)

## Topic worksheet

- Ask pupils if they can think of a castle in a film or cartoon. Can they describe it and who lives there? Pre-teach: *king, enemies, soldiers, holes, arrows, boiling oil, play tricks on.* Pupils read the text and underline three things they find interesting. They can use the labelled photo to help them with vocabulary. Pupils then look at the words for parts of a castle. In class pupils talk about what they know about the parts of a castle and what they found interesting.
- ***Optional follow-up activity:*** Pupils draw and label a 'fantasy' castle they would like to live in. How is the castle protected from enemies? Pupils show and describe their castles to the class or display them on the walls.

# Unit 3 Reinforcement worksheet 1

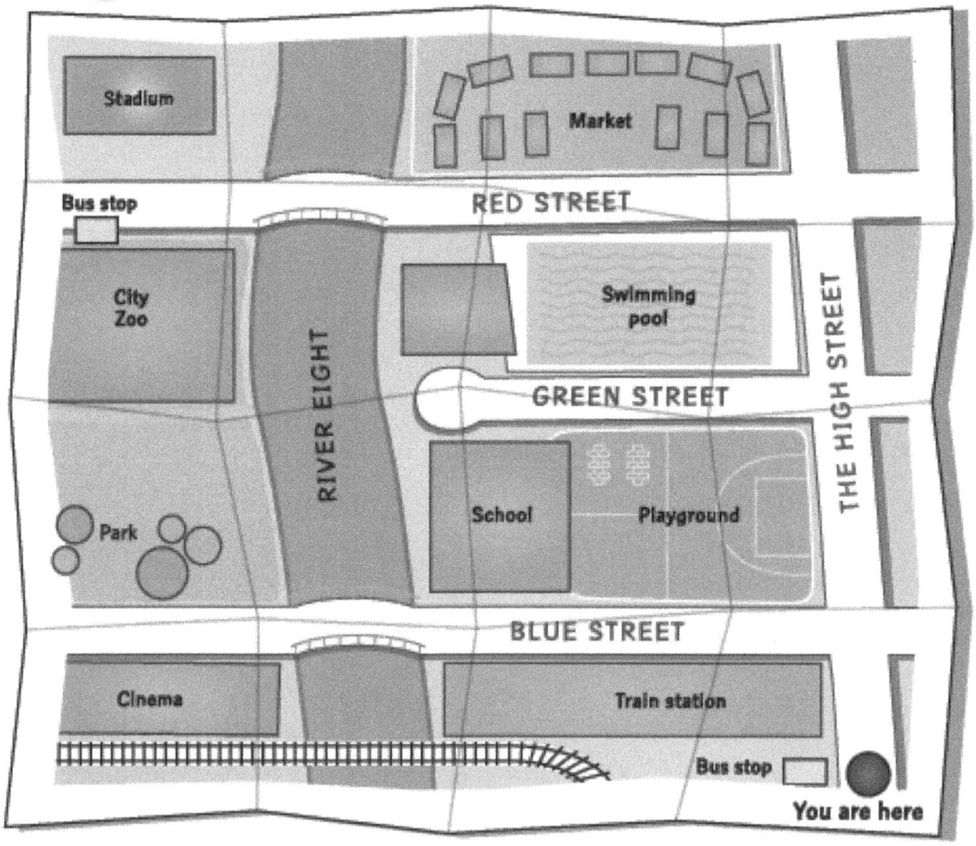


**Find *You are here* on the map. Circle the correct words.**

1 *Excuse me. Where's the playground?*

Go straight on and turn into Blue Street. The playground is on the corner. It's (opposite) / next to the train station.

2 *Excuse me. Where's the park?*

Go along the High Street. Take the first street on the left. Walk across / past the school. Cross the bridge and the park is on the right.

3 *Excuse me. Where's the swimming pool?*

Go along the High Street and turn left into Green Street. The swimming pool's on the right / left.

4 *Excuse me. Can you help me? Where's the cinema?*

Go straight on and take the first / second street on the left. Walk past the train station and across the bridge. It's on the left.

5 *Excuse me. Can you help me? I'm looking for the zoo.*

Go along the High Street. Take the second / third street on the left. Go past the swimming pool. Cross the river. It's on the left.

 

Unit 3

# Reinforcement worksheet 2

## 1 Find the words and label the pictures.

| | | | |
|---|---|---|---|
| sbu tops | bus stop | letho | |
| retrasuant | | iraropt | |
| xait | | tereath | |
| tasidum | | stop cffioe | |
| styiivuner | | uumems | |
| csalet | | ocelpi atstino | |

## 2 Some treasure is hidden in one of these places. Complete the answers to the clues to find out where it is!

1 People come here to learn. s [c] h o o l

2 We visit the _ [ ] _ _ to get money.

3 We go to the _ _ [ ] _ _ _ _ _ _ _ to buy stamps.

4 We go to the [ ] _ _ _ _ _ _ _ to watch plays.

5 When we are not at home, we often sleep in a _ _ _ _ [ ].

6 We go to a _ _ _ [ ] _ _ to look at old things that tell us about history.

**The treasure is in the** c _ _ _ _ _ **!**

  

Unit 3

# Extension worksheet 1

## 1 Use the words in brackets to complete the sentences.

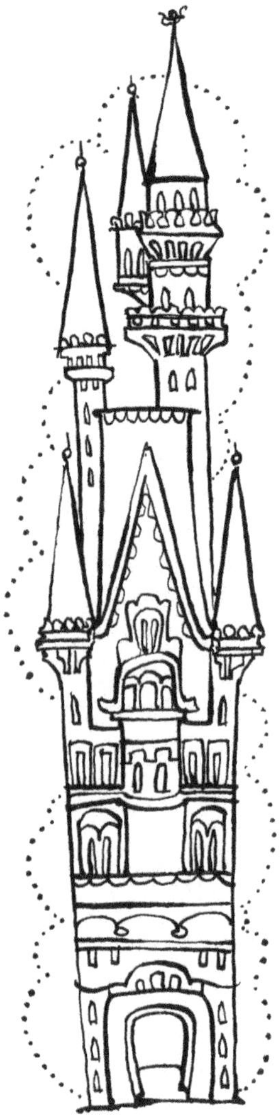

1 The world's ......biggest...... (big) train station is The Grand Central Terminal in New York, USA.

2 The ..most expensive.. (expensive) taxi ride in the world was a trip from London to Africa!

3 The .................... (large) palace in the world is owned by a very rich man, the Sultan of Brunei.

4 The world's .................... (small) museum is in the USA.

5 The .................... (fast) flight across the Atlantic Ocean took 1 hour, 54 minutes, 56.4 seconds.

6 One of the .................... (beautiful) castles in the world is in Prague.

7 The world's .................... (interesting) hotel is the Ice Hotel in Sweden. It's very cold inside!

8 The .................... (old) stamp is called a Penny Black.

## 2 Find more information about sentences 1–8.

a People first used it on their letters in 1840. ....8....

b More than 550 trains use it every day. ..........

c It has only one room! ..........

d His home has 1,778 rooms and 257 toilets. ..........

e It has an ice theatre and an ice church. ..........

f The passenger paid 62,908 US dollars! ..........

g It is also the biggest castle in the world. ..........

h The pilots flew from New York to London. ..........

Unit 3

# Extension worksheet 2

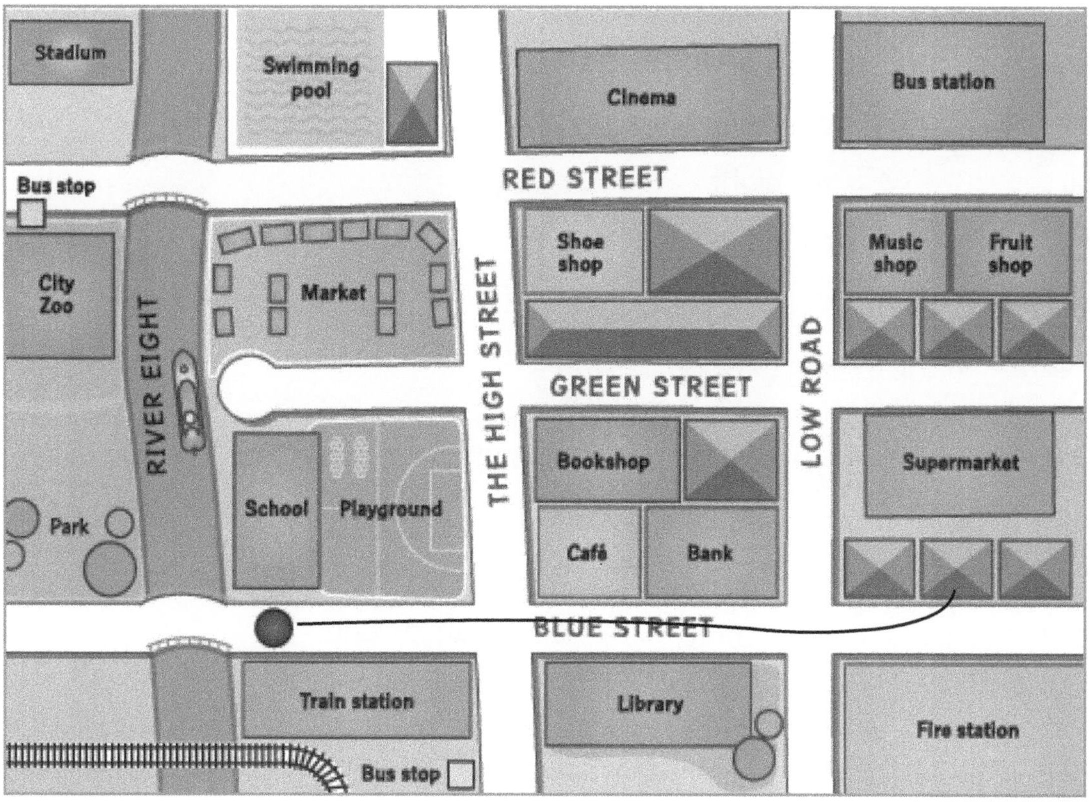


**1** **Look at the map and listen to Sally. She is talking about how she gets home from school. Then listen to the other children. Draw how they get home in these colours. The first one has been done for you.**

| | | | | | |
|---|---|---|---|---|---|
| Sally | ➔ | black | Fred | ➔ | green |
| Ben | ➔ | blue | Jim | ➔ | brown |
| Helen | ➔ | red | | | |

**2** My house is on Green Street next to the bookshop. Can you write how to get there from the school?

Katy

---------------------------------------------

---------------------------------------------

---------------------------------------------

---------------------------------------------

---------------------------------------------

---------------------------------------------

  

Unit 3

# Song worksheet

## 1 Match the rhyming words.

| | | | |
|---|---|---|---|
| 1 | hotel | a | too |
| 2 | day | b | eight |
| 3 | zoo | c | tell |
| 4 | street | d | play |
| 5 | late | e | eat |

## 2 Complete the song with the rhyming words.

Theatre, cinema,
Restaurant and hotel,
Museum, castle,
A story to ___tell___ .

I went to London,
To have a lovely day.
To go to a museum and
The theatre for a ________ .

I saw Tower Bridge,
And the castle ________ ,
Walked in the park,
And went to the zoo.

I went to a restaurant,
On the corner of the street.
I sat outside and
I had something to ________ .

I took a taxi,
Because it was ________ .
My train was in the station.
It was half past eight.

Theatre, cinema,
Restaurant and ________ ,
Museum, castle,
A story to tell.

## 3 (8) Listen and check your answers. Then sing the song.

## 4 Look and tick (✓) the places he visited. Which places *didn't* he visit?

# Unit 3 Topic worksheet

## 1 Read about castles. Underline three interesting facts.

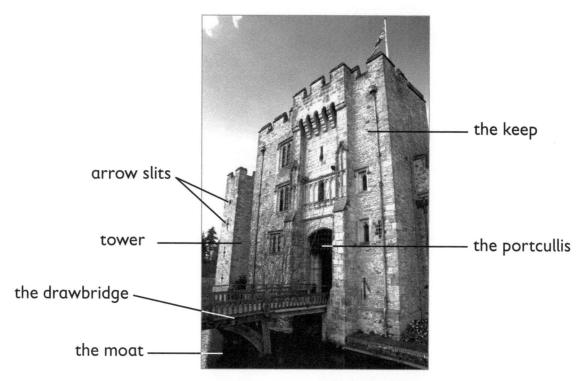

Hundreds of years ago, kings built castles to keep out their enemies. Sometimes thousands of soldiers lived inside the castle, usually in the **towers**. The king and his family usually lived in the **keep**.

Castles were strong. The walls were very thick and there were strong gates and a **portcullis** at the door. It was difficult for the enemy to break the gates and walls.

Castles were often on a hill. Why? Firstly, it was difficult for enemies to climb the hill. Secondly, it was easy for the soldiers in the castle to see their enemies from far away. Many castles had water (**a moat**) around them.

A castle with a moat also had a **drawbridge**. If the enemy came near the castle, the soldiers closed the drawbridge. Then their enemies could not cross the moat. Many people fell into the water. Then the soldiers sent arrows at the enemies from small holes in the towers (**arrow slits**).

If the enemies came into the castle, the soldiers played horrible tricks on them. For example, some castles had special floors which broke when the enemies came up the stairs. Castles also had **murder holes** (holes in the ceiling inside the keep). Soldiers waited at these places and threw boiling oil onto their enemies.

## 2 What do you know about these parts of a castle?

towers, moat, drawbridge, keep, arrow slits, portcullis, murder holes

## Reinforcement worksheet 1

- Pupils fill in the sentences with *was/were* and the past simple of the verb in brackets. They then match the sentences to the pictures. Finally they draw a picture of something that happened to them and write a sentence about it using the past simple and past continuous.

**Key: 1)** 2 were/arrived, 3 was/hurt, 4 was/started, 5 were/saw, 6 was/dropped, 7 were/came. **2)** (clockwise from example) 1, 5, 2, 7, 6, 4, 3.

- ***Optional follow-up activity:*** Pupils act out one of the sentences. The class guesses the sentence. Help with any necessary corrections in use of tenses.

## Reinforcement worksheet 2

- If necessary, review ordinal numbers. Pupils answer the questions about the times of the year. Then pupils work out the 'disaster' words based on the positions of the letters in the alphabet and the clues.

**Key: 1)** 2 August, 3 October, 4 December, 5 July, 6 April, 7 summer, 8 autumn. **2)** 2 earthquake, 3 storm, 4 iceberg, 5 tsunami, 6 volcano.

- ***Optional follow-up activity:*** Pupils write similar clues for their classmates to test months of the year, 'disaster' words and ordinal numbers.

## Extension worksheet 1

- Pupils use the pictures to choose the correct words for each sentence. Model the first one with pupils and then let them continue on their own. Finally, pupils copy out the sentences paying attention to spelling and punctuation.

**Key:** I was giving the bird some food when a mouse ran past. The cat was running after the mouse when the dog woke up. The dog was jumping on the cat when it hit me. We were going to the hospital when I remembered that the bird was still hungry!

- ***Optional follow-up activity:*** Pupils prepare their own sentence mazes for each other to practise past continuous and past simple.

## Extension worksheet 2

- Cut the photocopied worksheet in half. Elicit/pre-teach: *tsunami, volcano, ocean, steam, magma, rocks, fire, erupt.* Explain that the *Code* system helps scientists to know about these disasters before they happen and how dangerous they are going to be. The different colour codes mean different levels of danger. Pupils work in pairs for this information exchange activity. Pupil A begins. He/She tells his/her partner about the three warning stages of a tsunami. Pupil B listens and draws pictures to illustrate what happens in the appropriate boxes. Then Pupil B tells her/his partner about each of the warning stages of a volcano while Pupil A draws.
- ***Optional follow-up activity:*** Pupils imagine that they are journalists and write news reports about an erupting volcano or an imminent tsunami. They can use the information on the worksheet to explain what scientists did / are doing and what is happening / going to happen.

## Song worksheet

- Pupils read through the song once before you do actions for different lines of the song. Pupils shout out the line number. Then pupils listen to the song and cross out the extra word in each line.

**Key:** See Pupil's Book, page 37. The extra words are: 2 quickly, 3 heavy, 4 big, 5 slowly, 6 beautiful, 7 football, 8 chocolate, 9 all, 10 blue, 11 stone, 12 tall.

- ***Optional follow-up activity:*** Pupils play a Pictionary-style game in teams of two against two plus one judge. Each team writes four sentences using the past continuous and past simple, e.g. *I was swimming in a river when I saw a bear.* The two teams swap the sentences they have written. One pupil from each team picks a sentence and draws the meaning for their partner to guess the sentence. Then they swap roles and pick another sentence. The pair who guess all four sentences the quickest wins. The judge is there to time the pairs, to make sure no one cheats and to say who wins.

## Topic worksheet

- Introduce the topic by asking if pupils know any stories about floods, e.g. *Noah's Ark*. Explain that they are going to read four famous 'flood' stories (if possible, bring a map of the world so that you can show them where the stories come from). Pre-teach: *destroy, survive, greedy.* Pupils read the stories and label the pictures 1–4. As a class, discuss the question at the end of the text.

**Key:** The order of the pictures is as follows: a 2, b 1, c 4, d 3.

- ***Optional follow-up activity:*** Tell your pupils a very old/traditional story that you know. Then ask them if they can tell you one.

Unit 4

# Reinforcement worksheet 1

**1 Complete the sentences with *was* or *were* and the past of the word in brackets.**

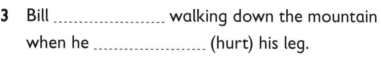

1 I ___was___ sailing in my boat when the storm ___began___ (begin).

2 You ________ talking to your friends when the taxi ________ (arrive).

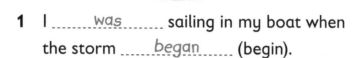

3 Bill ________ walking down the mountain when he ________ (hurt) his leg.

4 I ________ acting in a play when I ________ (start) to cough.

5 They ________ swimming in the sea when the shark ________ (see) them.

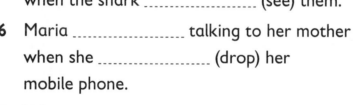

6 Maria ________ talking to her mother when she ________ (drop) her mobile phone.

7 We ________ having a picnic when the rain ________ (come).

**2 Write the numbers of the sentences next to the pictures.**

**3 Draw a picture and write a sentence about something that happened to you. Use *was/were + ing* and the past.**

____________________

____________________

____________________

____________________

____________________

____________________

  

Unit 4

# Reinforcement worksheet 2

## 1 Answer the questions.

1 What's the third month after February? May

2 What's the second month after June? ______________

3 What's the seventh month after March? ______________

4 What's the month before January? ______________

5 What's the tenth month after September? ______________

6 What's the fifth month after November? ______________

7 What's the season after spring? ______________

8 What's the season before winter? ______________

## 2 Read the clues and use the code to write the disaster words.

1 This word begins with the eighth letter of the alphabet. It's a very strong and dangerous wind. h u r r i c a n e

2 This disaster happens when the earth moves. It begins and ends with the fifth letter of the alphabet. _ _ _ _ _ _ _ _ _ _

3 This weather word begins with the nineteenth, twentieth, and fifteenth letters of the alphabet. _ _ _ _ _

4 When it was sailing across the Atlantic Ocean in 1912, the Titanic hit one of these. It ends with the seventh letter of the alphabet. It was an _ _ _ _ _ _ _ _.

5 This word begins with the twentieth and nineteenth letters of the alphabet. It means a very big wall of seawater. _ _ _ _ _ _ _

6 This word begins with the twenty-second letter of the alphabet and ends with the fifteenth. It's a disaster when one of these erupts! _ _ _ _ _ _ _

Unit 4

# Extension worksheet 1

## 1 Look at the pictures and join the correct words in the sentences.

| | | | | | | | |
|---|---|---|---|---|---|---|---|
|  | gave | the bird | some food | | a bird | ran | |
| I | was giving | the mouse | some milk | when | a mouse | was running | past. |
| | give | the cat | some help | | a bat | runs | |

| | | | | | | |
|---|---|---|---|---|---|---|
|  | was running after | the bird | | the dog | woke | |
| The cat | ran after | the mouse | when | the cat | wakes | up. |
| | runs after | the cat | | the mouse | is waking | |

| | | | | | |
|---|---|---|---|---|---|
|  | jumped on | the mouse | | it hit | |
| The dog | jumps on | the cat | when | it was hitting | me. |
| | was jumping on | the dog | | it hits | |

| | | | | | | | |
|---|---|---|---|---|---|---|---|
|  | went | to the farm | | I remembered that | the dog | was still | |
| We | go | to the hospital | when | I remember that | the bird | is still | hungry! |
| | were going | to the cinema | | I am remembering that | the cat | is still being | |

## 2 Copy the sentences from the story. Be careful with your spelling!

Unit 4

# Extension worksheet 2

**Pupil A – Tell your partner about the warning stages of a *tsunami.* Then listen to your partner tell you about the warning stages of a *volcano* and draw pictures of them in the code yellow, orange and red boxes.**

| TSUNAMI | CODE YELLOW<br>watch carefully | CODE ORANGE<br>very dangerous | CODE RED<br>disaster! |
|---|---|---|---|
| 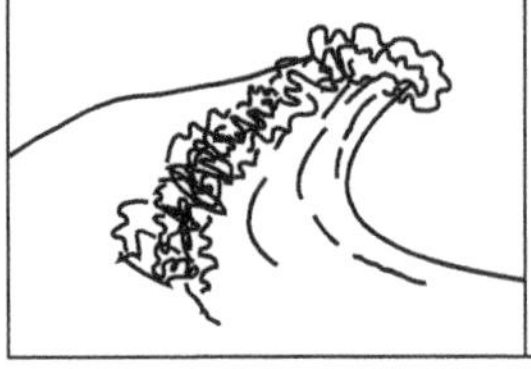 | A tsunami is possible. Scientists are looking at their computers. | There is an earthquake under the ocean. There is going to be a tsunami in 6–9 hours. | People who live near the sea must leave their homes. Soon there is going to be a very big wave. |

| VOLCANO | CODE YELLOW<br>watch carefully | CODE ORANGE<br>very dangerous | CODE RED<br>disaster! |
|---|---|---|---|
| 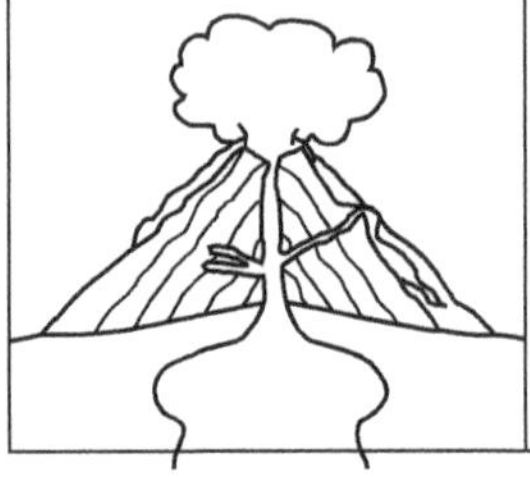 | | | |

**Pupil B – Listen to your partner tell you about the warning stages of a *tsunami* and draw pictures of them in the code yellow, orange and red boxes. Then tell your partner about the warning stages of a *volcano.***

| TSUNAMI | CODE YELLOW<br>watch carefully | CODE ORANGE<br>very dangerous | CODE RED<br>disaster! |
|---|---|---|---|
|  | | | |

| VOLCANO | CODE YELLOW<br>watch carefully | CODE ORANGE<br>very dangerous | CODE RED<br>disaster! |
|---|---|---|---|
| 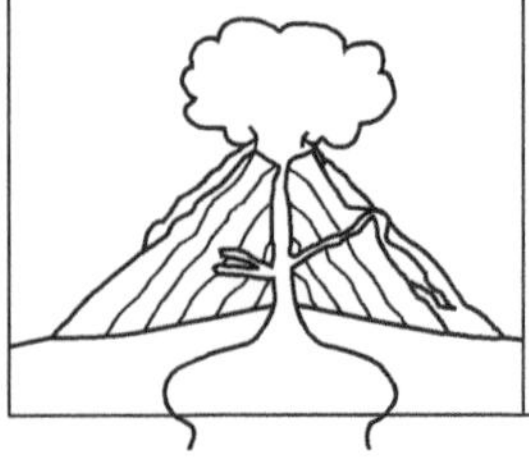 | Scientists can see on their computers that the volcano is starting to move. There is steam coming out of the top. | The volcano is beginning to erupt. Magma is starting to come out of the top. | The volcano is erupting. It's very dangerous. It is throwing rocks and fire out of the top. People have to leave their homes. |

 

Unit 4

# Song worksheet

**1 Read the song. Which line is your teacher acting?**

**2 9 Listen and cross out the extra word in each line.**

1 What were you doing when the ~~crazy~~ storm began?

2 When the lightning hit and the water ran quickly.

3 Where were you when the heavy rain came down?

4 On the mountain, at the beach, in the forest or the big town.

5 I was walking slowly up the mountain,

6 He was skating over the beautiful lake,

7 We were playing football in the park,

8 She was eating a piece of chocolate cake.

9 They were all swimming in the river,

10 He was sailing on the blue sea,

11 She was climbing up a stone wall,

12 I was sitting under a tall tree.

# Unit 4 Topic worksheet

**1 In many countries there are stories about a lot of rain and a big flood that destroyed almost everyone on Earth. Read the stories and label the pictures 1–4.**

a

b

c

d

1 **Ivory Coast, Africa**
A good, kind man gave everything he had to the animals. Then he gave his last meal to the god Ouende. Ouende thanked the good man and told him to leave his home. Then Ouende sent six months of rain to destroy all the bad people. Today all the people of the world are from the family of the good man.

3 **Siberia, Asia**
The rain didn't stop for seven days. Some people and animals survived the flood because they climbed trees. Other people moved to different places. This is why people speak different languages today.

2 **Philippines, Asia**
Water covered the whole Earth. Only two men and a woman survived. They went to sea. A great bird carried them on its back to their new homes.

4 **Guyana, South America**
Soon after people arrived on Earth, all food grew on one tree. Makunaima and his four brothers cut down the tree. Water poured from the tree and there were lots of fish in the water. One of the brothers tried to stop the water because he was worried about a flood. But Makunaima was greedy and he wanted more fish. So the water flooded the Earth.

**2 If people in different countries tell this story, do you think there was a big flood? What parts of the stories do you think are true?**

## Reinforcement worksheet 1

- Pre-teach: *cocoa beans, jungle, smell, cotton*. Pupils read the advertisement and complete the gaps with the *made of* structures provided. Then they unscramble and answer the questions. Pupils talk about question 3.

**Key: 1)** 2 is not / isn't made of, 3 is made of, 4 are made of, 5 are not / aren't made of, 6 are made of. **2)** 1 What is the river made of? (chocolate) 2 What can you do in the afternoon? (go to Chocolate School) 3 What is chocolate made from? (cocoa beans).

- ***Optional follow-up activity:*** Pupils work in groups and write a similar advertisement for a Museum of Sweets.

## Reinforcement worksheet 2

- Look at the examples. Point out to pupils that we don't use - *s* on the end of adjectives, even with plural nouns. Pupils make noun phrases from the nouns and adjectives and number the pictures. They then read the description to find the *What is it?* object, using the alphabet number code.

**Key: 1)** 3 a plastic toy, 4 metal keys, 5 a silver ring, 6 a cardboard box, 7 glass bottles, 8 a gold crown, 9 wool sweaters. **2)** (From left to right) 4, 1, 9, 2, 7, 8. **3)** The object is **a wooden table**. Point out *wooden* not *wood*.

- ***Optional follow-up activity:*** In pairs, pupils give clues about the objects in the list e.g. where you put it / what you put in it / what you do with it / where you find it. Their partner guesses what the object is.

## Extension worksheet 1

- Pupils work out the missing word in each sentence and cross them out on the wall. Then they find three things that can be made with each of the four crossed out materials.

**Key:** 2 wool 3 paper, 4 wood, 5 nylon, 6 hair, 7 metal, 8 stone, 9 sand, 10 fur, 11 plastic. The line of crossed out words is: paper, wool, plastic, nylon.

- ***Optional follow-up activity:*** Pupils list which things are natural and which things we make. (Natural: *oil, wood, hair, stone, sand, fur, rubber, bone, wool*. Things we make: *glass, metal, paper, nylon, plastic, sugar, chocolate*.)

## Extension worksheet 2

F towards

- Pupils listen to the instructions, then colour and write. They need the following three colours: green, red, yellow.

**Key:** 1 green box containing comics, 2 PAPER written on left hand recycling bin, 3 yellow car nearest street corner, 4 red door next to man, 5 PLASTIC written on middle recycling bin.

**Audioscript.** FCH: Look at this picture of my family.
M: That's good, Daisy. What are they doing?
FCH: They're at the new recycling bins. My mum and my brothers are putting things in them.
M: This picture's in black and white. Do you want to colour it?
FCH: OK. I can colour my brother Nick's T-shirt.
M: Which boy is he?
FCH: He's putting a bottle into the bin on the right.
M: OK. Why don't you colour his T-shirt black?
*Can you see the black T-shirt? This is an example.*
*Now you listen and colour and write.*

1 M: Can you recycle lots of different things there?
FCH: Yes, my mum's holding a lot of things in her box.
M: And there's a box full of paper on the ground.
FCH: Our old comics are in that box. We've got lots!
M: You could colour that box green.
FCH: OK.

2 M: There's no writing on the big recycling bins.
FCH: I know. Shall I write on one of them?
M: You could write PAPER on that one on the left.
FCH: That's a good idea. I'm doing that now.

3 M: Your family has a lot of things to recycle.
FCH: Yes. And they're very heavy too. We took them to the recycling bins in the car.
M: Is your car in the picture?
FCH: Yes. It's the one nearest the corner. It's yellow. I love it.
M: Well, I think you should colour your car too.

4 M: Who's that man? Is that your dad?
FCH: No, it's my friend May's dad. He's standing by their front door. Shall I colour the door?
M: OK. What colour is their door?
FCH: It's red.
M: That's a nice colour. Yes, do that.

5 FCH: Can I write something else now?
M: Yes, of course. Can you see the bin in the middle?
FCH: Yes, I can. What's that for?
M: It's for plastic. Write that on the bin.
FCH: OK ... I've done that now!
M: Well done! That's a very nice picture of your family, Daisy.

- ***Optional follow-up activity:*** Pupils ask each other questions about the picture, e.g. *Where are the people? What are the houses made of?* or describe things for the others to guess, e.g. *The small boy's got it in his hand.*

## Song worksheet

- Pupils listen to the song and find materials + objects as in the example. Pupils then choose any three objects from the song, draw pictures and label them.

**Key:** a glass bowl, a wooden table, a grass skirt, a silver box, a gold watch, a wool scarf, paper books / card book covers.

- ***Optional follow-up activity:*** Write four columns on the board headed *metal, glass, wood, silver*. Elicit things made of each material and make lists on the board. Pupils replace the objects in the song. For example, instead of *This chair is made of metal*, they can write *This box is made of metal*.

## Topic worksheet

- Ask pupils to look at the picture of the landfill. What do they imagine is in there? Pre-teach: *rubbish, landfill, throw away, decompose, hot dogs, underground, crazy*. Pupils read the article and underline three interesting facts and discuss. Then pupils list ten things they and their family threw away this week.
- ***Optional follow-up activity:*** Pupils draw a landfill with the things that they throw away and label the objects inside it. In groups, they discuss their ideas for recycling them instead.

Unit 5

# Reinforcement worksheet 1

**1** **Read about the Museum of Chocolate! Complete the sentences with *is made of* / *isn't made of* / *are made of* / *aren't made of.***

## Museum of Chocolate

**Do you like chocolate? Would you like to learn how chocolate is made? Come to the Museum of Chocolate!**

You can see our museum by boat! You travel along the river and learn how chocolate is made. We have good boats, but don't fall in the river. The river (1) is made of chocolate!

Don't miss Chocolate School in the afternoon. If you like art, you can learn how to paint and write with chocolate! If you prefer geography, explore our jungle to find cocoa beans. Chocolate is made from cocoa beans. The jungle (2) ______________________ chocolate, but it smells beautiful!

Finally, don't forget to visit the Choc-Shop! Buy a present that (3) ______________________ chocolate. Our toys, pictures and books (4) ______________________ chocolate! But some presents in the Choc-Shop (5) ______________________ chocolate. The T-shirts, for example, (6) ______________________ cotton!

**2** **Write the questions. Then answer them.**

1 What / made / of / river / is / the / ?

______________________________________________

2 can / do / you / afternoon / the / in / ? / What

______________________________________________

3 chocolate / from / made / is / What / ?

______________________________________________

**3** **Which 'Chocolate School' class would you like to go to? Why?**

Unit 5

# Reinforcement worksheet 2

**1 If …** **we call it/them …**

1 a bag is made of paper, ........a paper bag........ .

2 shoes are made of leather, ........leather shoes........ .

3 a toy is made of plastic, ................................ .

4 keys are made of metal, ................................ .

5 a ring is made of silver, ................................ .

6 a box is made of cardboard, ................................ .

7 bottles are made of glass, ................................ .

8 a crown is made of gold, ................................ .

9 sweaters are made of wool, ................................ .

**2 Number the pictures.**

4

☐

☐

☐

☐

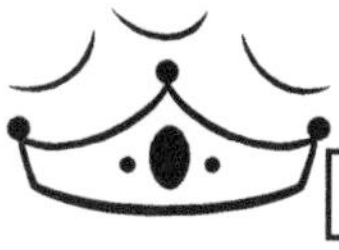
☐

**3 What is it? Read the description and use the code.**

It is made of wood. It is in your classroom and in your house.
And you use it every day when you write and eat!

| A | B | C | D | E | F | G | H | I | J | K | L | M | N | O | P | Q | R | S | T | U | V | W | X | Y | Z |
|---|---|---|---|---|---|---|---|---|---|---|---|---|---|---|---|---|---|---|---|---|---|---|---|---|---|
| 1 | 2 | 3 | 4 | 5 | 6 | 7 | 8 | 9 | 10 | 11 | 12 | 13 | 14 | 15 | 16 | 17 | 18 | 19 | 20 | 21 | 22 | 23 | 24 | 25 | 26 |

_   _ _ _ _ _ _   _ _ _ _ _

1   23 15 15 4 5 14   20 1 2 12 5

Unit 5

# Extension worksheet 1

## 1 Complete the sentences and cross out the materials on the wall.

1 Bottles are usually made of plastic or ......glass...... .

2 We get .................... from sheep.

3 This worksheet is made of .................... .

4 Paper and card are made from .................... !

5 The word .................... comes from the names of two cities: New York and London.

6 Fur comes from animal .................... .

7 Gold and silver are two types of .................... .

8 Castles were often made of .................... , wood or brick.

9 Glass is made from a kind of .................... .

10 Very warm clothes can be made of wool or .................... .

11 Pens and rulers are usually made of .................... .

| | | | |
|---|---|---|---|
| ~~glass~~ | hair | stone | bone |
| sugar | oil | chocolate | fur |
| paper | wool | plastic | nylon |
| wood | metal | rubber | sand |

## 2 Which four crossed out materials form a line? Write three things you can make with each of them.

1 .................... : .................... .................... ....................

2 .................... : .................... .................... ....................

3 .................... : .................... .................... ....................

4 .................... : .................... .................... ....................

Unit 5

# Extension worksheet 2

10 **Listen to Daisy. She's talking to her teacher. Colour the things you hear in the picture and write.**

Unit 5

# Song worksheet

## 1 (11) Listen and read. Write 8 of the things in verses 2, 3 and 4.

1 a metal chair

2 ..................

3 ..................

4 ..................

5 ..................

6 ..................

7 ..................

8 ..................

1 Everything's material,
Everything we see.
From rocks, plants or animals,
Or from a factory.

2 This chair is made of metal,
That bowl is made of glass.
This table's made of wood,
And that skirt's made of grass.

3 This box is made of silver,
That watch is made of gold.
This scarf is made of wool,
And I wear it when it's cold.

4 Books are made of paper,
Their covers are made of card.
Some things are made of plastic,
Which can be strong and hard.

## 2 Draw three things from the song. Colour and label them.

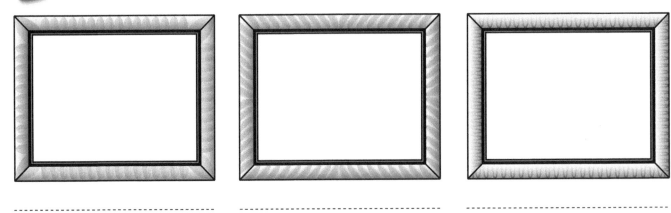

.................. .................. ..................

 

Unit 5

# Topic worksheet

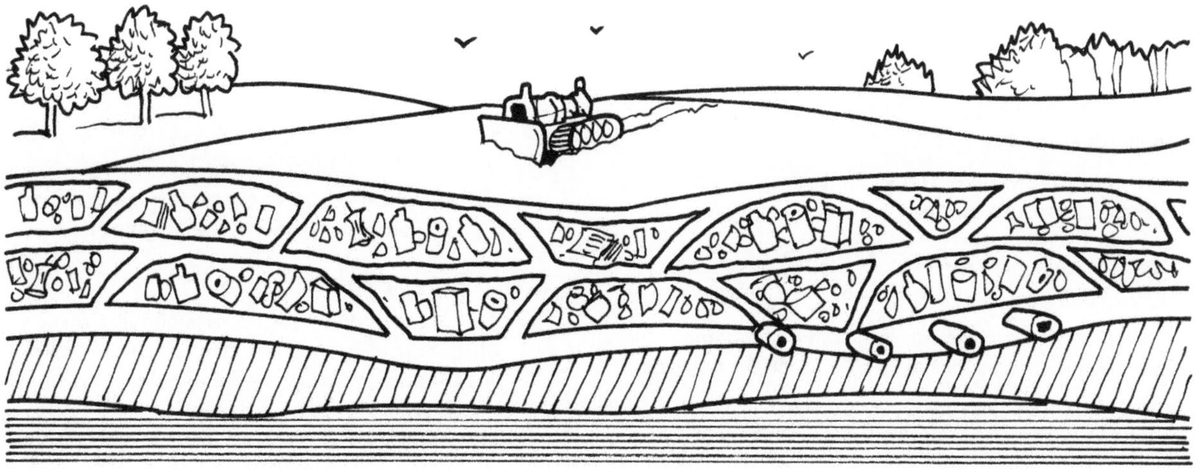

Landfill – a place where rubbish is buried underground

## 1 Read about landfills. Underline 3 interesting facts.

Imagine you are an archaeologist, but not one like Diggory Bones. He digs up bones and studies people from a long time ago. You study our rubbish now! Every day we throw away lots of things, like paper, metal, plastic and grass. So you dig up the places where we put our rubbish, *landfills*, to see what's inside!

Would you like to look at our rubbish under the ground? It's very interesting. When one archaeologist dug up landfills in the USA, he found some old newspapers. He was surprised because they were 30 years old but he could still read them! He also found five hot dogs. But he didn't eat them!

The archaeologist found out that some things take much longer to decompose than he thought. He found grass, for example, which was not yellow. It was still green after many years.

This is a problem. There isn't very much more space underground for our rubbish. We put a lot of paper in landfills. This is crazy, because it is easy to recycle. If we recycle paper, there's more space underground for things we can't recycle. So please don't throw paper away!

## 2 Make a list of ten things that you and your family threw away this week.

---------------------------------------------- ----------------------------------------------
---------------------------------------------- ----------------------------------------------
---------------------------------------------- ----------------------------------------------
---------------------------------------------- ----------------------------------------------
---------------------------------------------- ----------------------------------------------

## Reinforcement worksheet 1

- Tell pupils that it is Mary's birthday and her friends are playing a game. She is blindfolded and she has to guess what her presents are. Pupils read the three dialogues and complete the sentences, using the words in each cake.

**Key:** 1 sounds, What, bottle, 2 like, soft, feels, look, 3 Smell, smells, does, tastes.

- ***Optional follow-up activity:*** Pupils practise the dialogues in groups of four.

## Reinforcement worksheet 2

F towards

- Pupils tick the words that they see in the drawing. They then read the clues and write in the food words.

**Key: 1)** Words not ticked should be: spoon, sausage, salt, onions. **2)** 2 salt, 3 spoon, 4 pepper, 5 knife, 6 fork, 7 olives, 8 meal.

- ***Optional follow-up activity:*** Pupils draw, colour and label their favourite meals. You could make a chart showing which meals are most/least popular in the class and stick their pictures around it. You may need to help them with some more food vocabulary.

## Extension worksheet 1

- Pupils describe the clouds, using the expression *look(s) like*. Then pupils match the questions and answers. Point out: *feel like / smell like / taste like / sound like*.

**Key: 1)** (possible answers) 1 boat, 2 like a bottle, 3 This cloud looks like an elephant, 4 This cloud looks like a shoe.
**2)** 2 What does it taste like? 3 What does it feel like? 4 What does it sound like? 5 What does it smell like? 6 What does it feel like? What does it taste like?

- ***Optional follow-up activity:*** Pupils draw pictures of clouds and show them to their partner. What do they look like? Encourage pupils to use their imagination! If possible, bring in different smelling, tasting and feeling objects. Put them in a bag or blindfold pupils if they are food, for them to describe what they smell, feel, taste, sound like etc.

## Extension worksheet 2

- Pupils read the steps for making a sandwich and put them in order. Then pupils write down six steps for making their favourite kind of sandwich. Ask them to cut along the dotted lines and give all of their sentences mixed up to their partner. The partner puts the steps in order.

**Key:** 4, 6, 2, 5, 3, 1, 7.

- ***Optional follow-up activity:*** Pupils put their sandwich recipes on the wall. They read each other's recipes and choose their favourite one. Suggest that for homework they make one of their friends' favourite sandwiches.

## Song worksheet

- Pupils match the words to the pictures and then write the words in the gaps. They listen to the song to check their answers.

**Key: 1)** Clockwise from example: a, f, d, n, c, i, k, g, h, m, b, l, e, j. **2)** See Pupil's Book, page 57.

- ***Optional follow-up activity:*** Pupils invent actions to go with the song and perform them while singing.

## Topic worksheet

- Pupils read about animal senses and find three ways in which humans' senses are different. Pupils colour the boxes containing things we eat and drink with red, food words green, drinks words blue and the senses yellow. The picture will reveal a red flower on grass with a blue sky and a sun on the top right. Note: The picture is blurred or unclear because insects can't see shapes of objects as clearly as humans can.

**Key:** Human senses are different because we touch with our fingers, not our noses, we can't hear very high sounds, we can't smell danger like some animals, our eyes see differently.

**Colour code:** green (food) – eggs, tomato, salt, cheese, salad, meat, bread; blue (drinks) – water, juice, milk, cola; red (things we eat and drink with) – knife, fork, spoon, bowl, plate, glass; yellow (senses) – touch, taste, hearing.

- ***Optional follow-up activity:*** Pupils discuss what is the most important sense for them and why.

Unit 6

# Reinforcement worksheet 1

**It's Mary's birthday. Her friends are playing a game. She has to guess what her presents are. Complete the sentences.**

**1**

**Sue:** Mary! Listen to this! What does it ......*sound*...... like?

**Mary:** Mmmm. It .................... like water.

**Sue:** Now smell it! .................... does it smell like?

**Mary:** It smells like flowers! I think it's a .................... of perfume.

**2**

**Dan:** It's my turn. Touch this! What does it feel .................... ?

**Mary:** It feels like a .................... bowl.

**Dan:** But it's not a bowl! You put it on your head!

**Mary:** It .................... like a hat. Is it a hat?

**Dan:** Yes it is! And you're going to .................... like a film star in it!

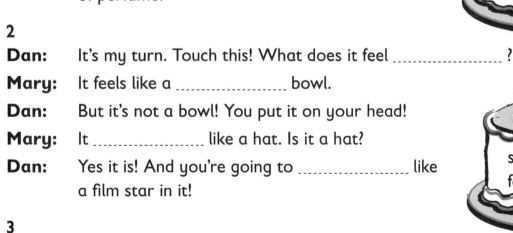

**3**

**John:** .................... this! What is it, Mary?

**Mary:** It .................... like chocolate.

**John:** Now taste it! What .................... it taste like?

**Mary:** It .................... creamy. It's a cake. I know, it's my birthday cake!

**John:** Yes, it is! And here's a fork and a plate, so you can eat it!

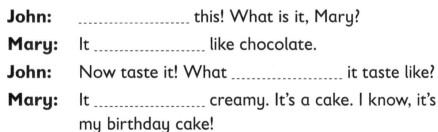

  

Unit 6

# Reinforcement worksheet 2

## 1 Tick (✓) the things that you can see in Amy's meal.

| | |
|---|---|
| fork | ✓ |
| flour | |
| spoon | |
| sausage | |
| cheese | |
| pepper | |
| salt | |
| tomato | |
| onions | |
| pizza | |
| plate | |
| knife | |
| olives | |

## 2 Read the clues and write the words.

1 It's made of wheat. We use it to make bread and pizza. f l o u r
2 It's white and you use it to make your food taste good. _ _ _ _
3 It's something we use to eat soup or cereal. _ _ _ _ _
4 It's black and it tastes strong. _ _ _ _ _ _
5 It's made of metal. We use it to cut our food. _ _ _ _ _
6 We use it to bring food from our plate to our mouth. _ _ _ _
7 They're small green or black fruits and they taste strong. _ _ _ _ _
8 It's what we call breakfast, lunch and dinner. _ _ _ _

Unit 6

# Extension worksheet 1

**1 Look at the clouds. They have interesting shapes. What do you think each one looks like?**

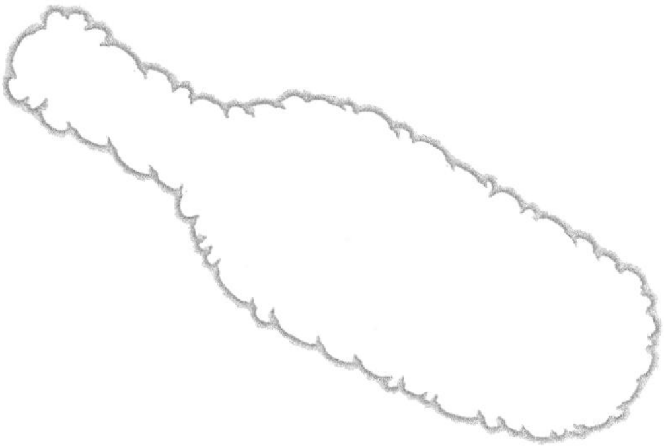

1 This cloud looks like a ..................

..................................................

2 This cloud looks ..................

..................................................

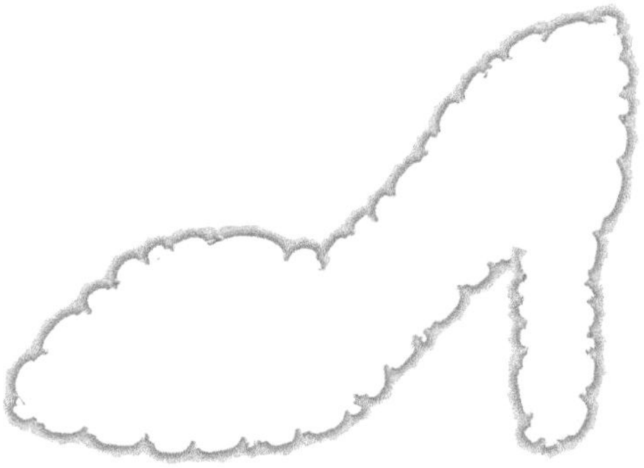

3 ..................................................

..................................................

4 ..................................................

..................................................

**2 Complete the questions and the answers.**

1 What ....*does it smell*.... like? It ....*smells like a*.... flower.

2 What .................................. like? It .................................. sugar.

3 What .................................. like? It .................................. fur.

4 What .................................. like? It .................................. French.

5 What .................................. like? It .................................. paint.

6 What .................................. like? It .................................. plastic.

Unit 6

# Extension worksheet 2

**1 This is how I make my favourite sandwich. Number the steps.**

........... Then I spread strawberry jam on top of the peanut butter.

........... Then I cut them in half.

........... First I take two pieces of bread.

........... Then I put the two pieces of bread together.

........... Next, I put peanut butter on both pieces of bread.

.....1..... Ingredients: two pieces of bread, strawberry jam and peanut butter.

........... Finally, I eat my sandwich!

**2 Write down six steps for making your favourite kind of sandwich. Then cut along the dotted lines and give all of your sentences to your partner. Ask your partner to put the steps in order.**

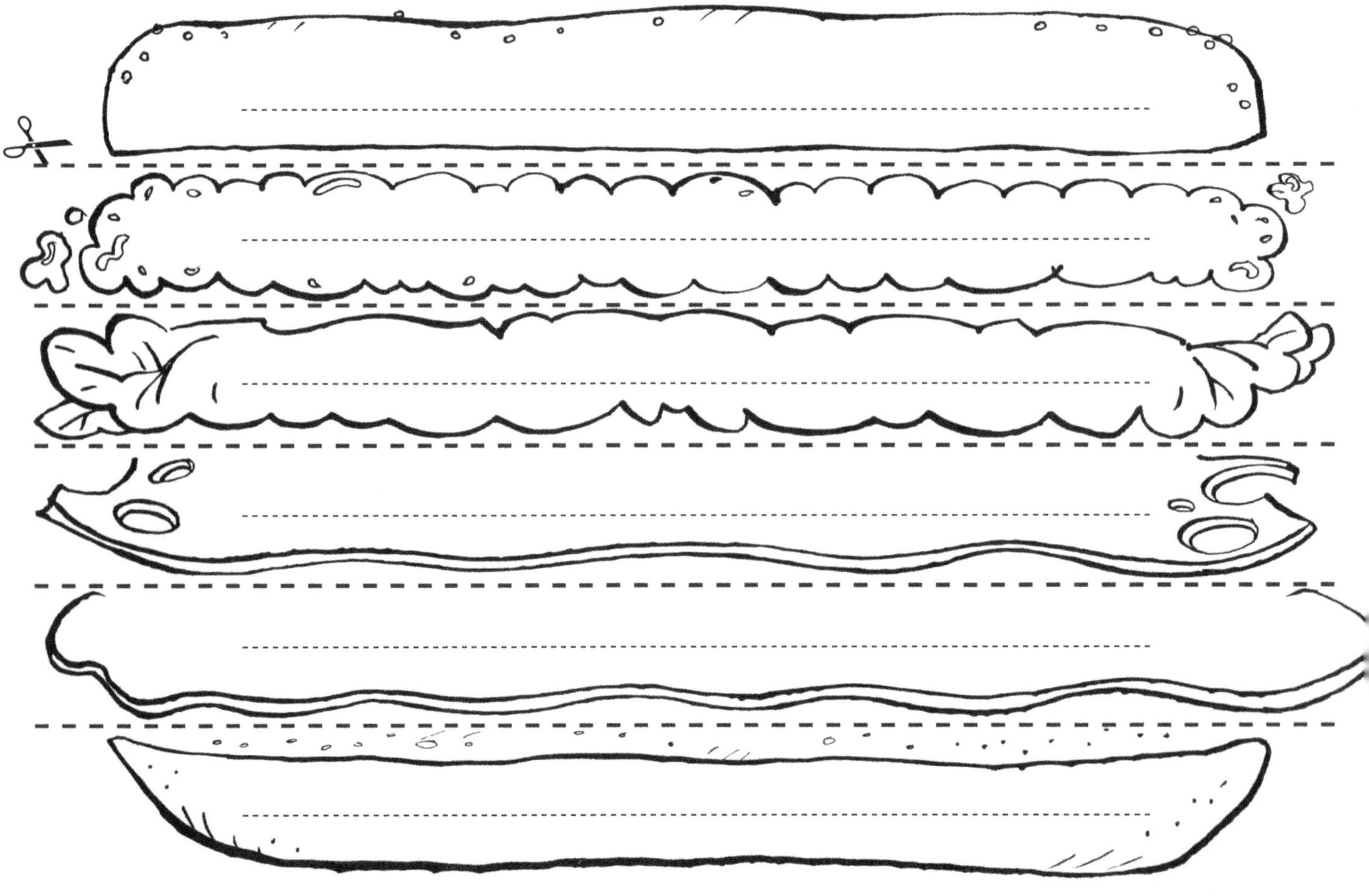

Unit 6

# Song worksheet

## 1 Match the words with the pictures.

| | | | | | | |
|---|---|---|---|---|---|---|
| a ~~Mario~~ | b wait | c cheese | d onion | e plate | f throw | g tastes |
| h hair | i knife | j hands | k bowl | l flour | m pizza | n listen |

## 2 Complete the song with the words.

a

My name's Mario ,
I'm an Italian cook.
If you want to make a p.................. ,
Then l.................. to me and look.

Take salt, yeast, f.................. and water,
Put them in a b.................. .
Mix them all together,
And w.................. for it to grow.

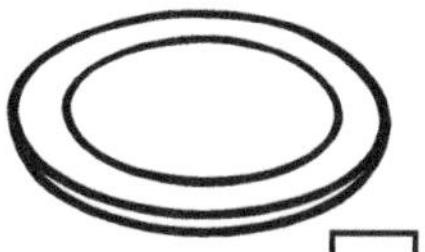

When the base is bigger,
Th.................. it in the air.
Use your h.................. to turn it,
Don't get it in your h.................. .

Now you choose your topping,
Tomato, pepper and ch.................. .
You can choose anything,
Sausage, o.................. and meat.

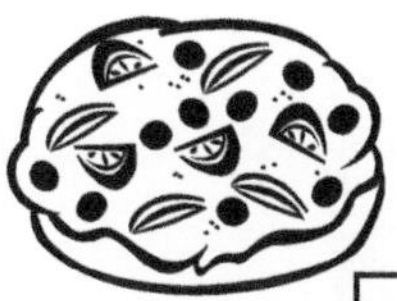

Cook for 15 minutes,
Then put it on a p.................. .
Cut it with a k.................. and fork,
Mmm. Now that.................. great!

## 3 12 Listen to the song and check your answers.

 

Unit 6

# Topic worksheet

**Read about the senses. Find three ways in which our senses are different to those of animals.**

## The Five Senses

The five senses are: touch, taste, hearing, smell and sight. Humans usually have all five senses but they are not the same as the senses of other animals. Think about touch. Humans touch things with their fingers, but small animals touch with their noses. What about taste? Snakes can taste food better than us! And hearing? Bats and dogs can hear very high sounds that humans can't hear. And humans can't smell danger like some animals. We can smell meat, but lions can smell it much better. They need to find and eat it!

Now think about sight. Humans see objects very differently from insects. Insects can't see objects very well. Their eyes are different from our eyes because they need to see movements and colours that we don't need. What does a red flower look like to you? To find out what a red flower looks like to an insect, colour all the boxes with things we eat with and drink with in red in the picture. Now colour the boxes with types of food in green. This is what green grass looks like to an insect.

Now colour the drinks boxes in blue and the senses in yellow. These are what the sun and the sky look like to an insect.

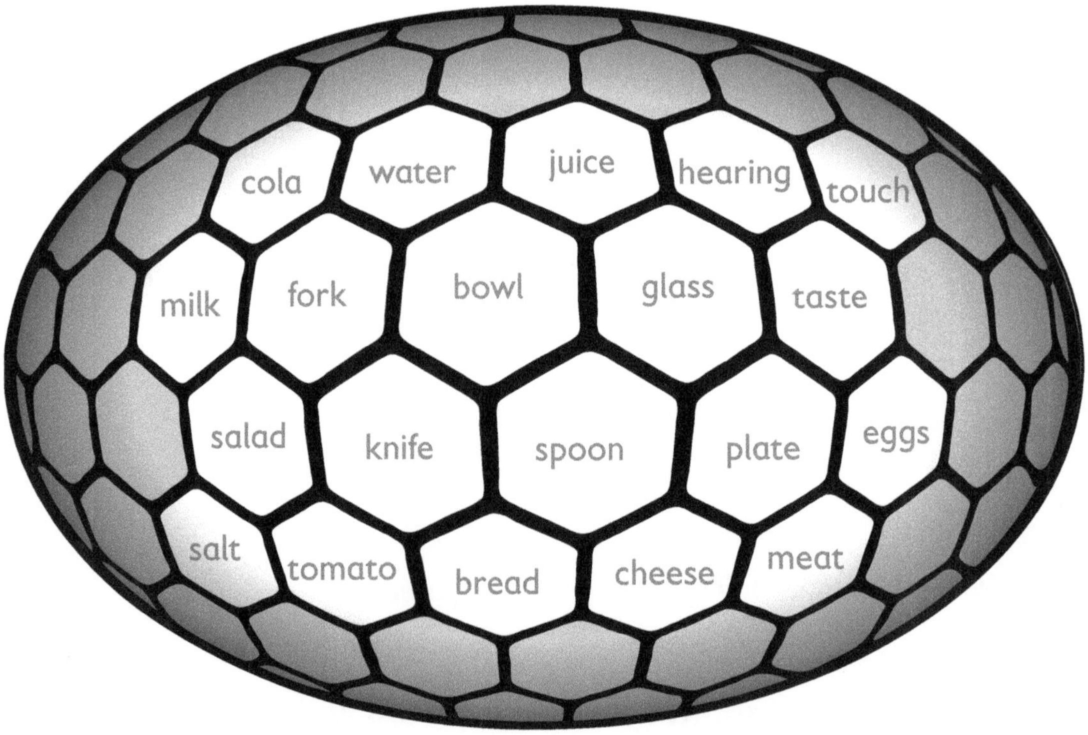

## Reinforcement worksheet 1

- Pupils complete the statements and questions using *should(n't)* + the verb given in brackets. Show pupils how to match the responses to these sentences by pointing out the example. They can then match the rest of the sentences on their own.

**Key: 1)** 2 should you do, 3 Should we run? 4 shouldn't walk, 5 shouldn't camp, 6 Should I tell, 7 should we put, 8 should we call? **2)** b 1, c 4, d 3, e 7, f 2, g 6, h 5.

- ***Optional follow-up activity:*** Pupils work in pairs and think about what they should do to keep themselves well and safe, for example, in the street or in the house. They make posters to put on the classroom wall for a *Keep Safe* campaign, using *should / shouldn't* sentences.

## Reinforcement worksheet 2

- Pupils complete the sentences. They can refer back to the Pupil's Book, page 66 to help them. Then they copy the letters they have written in the boxes to find a ten-letter mystery word.

**Key: 1)** 2 Nature, 3 extinct, 4 wings, 5 Butterflies, 6 spots, 7 striped, 8 species, 9 insects, 10 collect. **2)** The mystery word is **rainforest**.

- ***Optional follow-up activity:*** Give a 10-minute time limit. In pairs or alone, pupils make as many words as they can out of *endangered species*. The words must be a minimum of four letters long. They should not use plurals.

## Extension worksheet 1

- Ask pupils if they know a nature park and introduce *The Bear Nature Park*. Elicit what pupils think you can do there. Explain that water fell on the instructions for visiting this park. Pupils read the instructions and fill in the missing words. Then they circle the eight words in the wordsearch.

**Key:** 2 thirsty, 3 hat, 4 rubbish, 5 shouldn't, 6 wings, 7 stripes, 8 your.

- ***Optional follow-up activity:*** Pupils write a set of instructions for a trip to the beach or the rainforest.

## Extension worksheet 2

F towards

- Photocopy the worksheet and cut each worksheet in half. Introduce the two types of butterfly and tell pupils that they are going to tell their partner some information about them. Write the prompts from the worksheet on the board and elicit the full questions: *What colour is your butterfly? How big are its wings? Where does it live? Can you tell me an interesting fact about your butterfly?* Ask pupils to sit in pairs, facing each other. Give one pupil in each pair the 'Pupil A' sheet and the other one 'Pupil B'. As this is an information exchange activity, tell them they should not look at each other's sheets. Pupils focus on the Zebra Swallowtail first. Pupil As ask the questions and write down Pupil Bs' answers. Then pupils change roles. Pupils then colour in the butterfly they have learned about using the information they've been given.

- ***Optional follow-up activity:*** Write useful words from the text without vowels on the board and ask pupils to come up and write the correct words e.g. *wng, spts, strps, bttrfly.* Pupils can then take turns to write up other words from the unit without vowels for the class to complete.

## Song worksheet

- Pupils decide on actions to go with each line of the song. Get them to demonstrate some of their 'moves' to the class. Play the song once and let them read the words and do the actions while they listen. Then play the song again. This time they have to listen only and do the appropriate actions, singing at the same time, if they can.

- ***Optional follow-up activity:*** Pupils work in pairs. They mime a line for another pair who have to guess the line from the song.

## Topic worksheet

- Pre-teach: *camouflage, feathers, tail, pattern, poison, hide, polar bear, leaves, feel sick* and *caterpillar.* Pupils read the article about camouflage. As they read, they choose a title for each paragraph. Then pupils look at the three pictures and talk or write about them. Help pupils by asking questions like: *What kind of animal is it? What colour is it? Can you describe its pattern? How does it hide from its enemies? What does the enemy think it is? What kind of camouflage does it use? (Colour, pattern, smell/poison, or all three?)*

**Key: 1)** 1 Colour, 2 Pattern, 3 Smells and poison.
**2)** butterfly – pattern and colour; caterpillar – pattern, colour, smells; frog – pattern, colour, possibly poison.

- ***Optional follow-up activity:*** Ask pupils to research *animal camouflage* on the internet. They should bring information on camouflage they have found to the next lesson and tell their classmates about it, either by speaking or writing. You can refer them to: http://animals.howstuffworks.com/animal-facts/animal-camouflage-pictures.htm

Unit 7

# Reinforcement worksheet 1

## 1 Complete the sentences with *should* / *shouldn't* and the words in brackets.

1 People shouldn't throw (not/throw) plastic bags in the lake.

2 What ____________ you ____________ (do) if you have a terrible toothache?

3 Oh no! There's a cow in the field. Is it going to come after us? ____________ we ____________ (run)?

4 Daisy's face is very red. She ____________ ____________ (not/walk) in this hot sun.

5 What's that man doing? He ____________ ____________ (not/camp) there.

6 I don't understand this English homework. ____________ I ____________ (tell) my teacher?

7 Where ____________ we ____________ (put) our rubbish?

8 Oh no! There's a fire! Who ____________ we ____________ (call)?

## 2 Find the answers to questions 1–8.

a Call the fire fighters. Quick! Here's my mobile phone! 8

b That's right. It's dangerous for the ducks and fish. ______

c You're right. She should put some sun cream on. ______

d No, don't run! Just don't walk too near it. ______

e In the rubbish bin, of course! ______

f You should go to the dentist. ______

g Of course you should. She can help you. ______

h Yes. It's not safe to put the tent there. ______

 

Unit 7

# Reinforcement worksheet 2

## 1 Complete each sentence with a word about the natural world.

1 Zebras have black and white s t [r] i p e s.
2 N [ ] _ _ _ _ is in danger because of people's actions.
3 Creatures, like the dinosaur, that die out are e _ _ [ ] _ _ _ .
4 Birds have w _ [ ] _ _ . They need them to fly.
5 B _ _ _ _ _ [ ] _ _ _ _ are beautiful. They can fly.
6 Many fish have round s _ [ ] _ _ on their body.
7 The Siberian tiger has a long s _ [ ] _ _ _ _ tail.
8 There are a thousand endangered s _ [ ] _ _ _ _ in the world.
9 Flies and beetles are examples of flying i _ [ ] _ _ _ _ .
10 People should not c _ _ _ _ _ [ ] fish to have in their homes.

## 2 Write the letters from the boxes in 1–10 to find a place where frogs live!

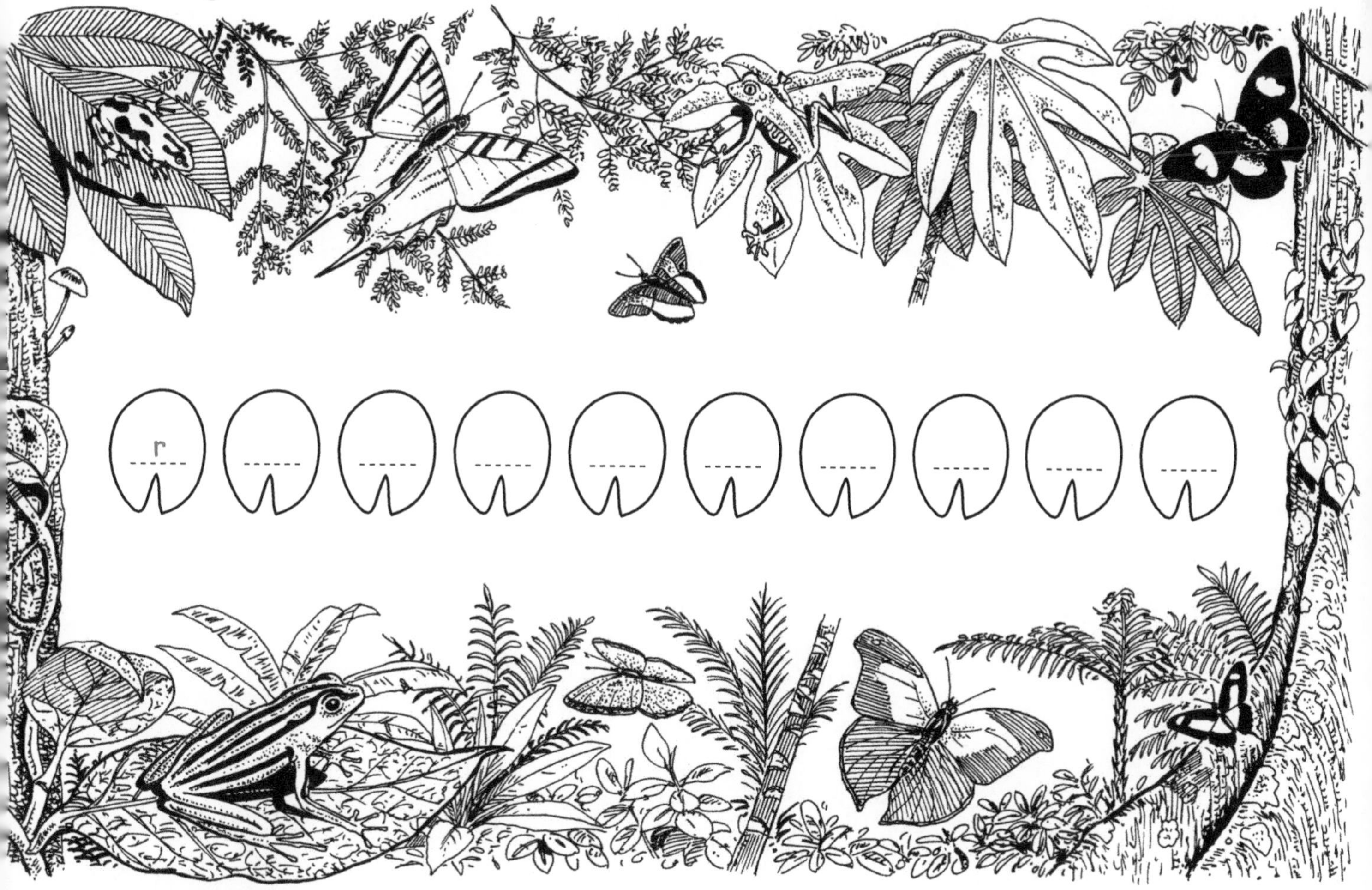


  

# Extension worksheet 1

**1** **These are the instructions for having a good and safe time in The Bear Nature Park. But some rain fell on them. Complete the instructions.**

## Welcome to The Bear Nature Park!

Please follow these simple instructions:

1. You should pack lots of bottles of *water* in your bag.
2. If you become ______, drink lots of water.
3. Wear your ______ when the sun is hot.
4. After your picnic, put your ______ in the bin.
5. You ______ throw plastic bags in the lake.
6. There are many spotted butterflies in the park. Please don't touch them. You can break their ______.
7. Lehmann's frogs have red ______ and they are poisonous. Don't touch them.
8. You should always stay with ______ friends!

**Enjoy your visit to The Bear Nature Park!**

**2** **Find and circle the 8 missing words.**

| | | | | | | | |
|---|---|---|---|---|---|---|---|
| s | t | r | i | p | e | s | r |
| d | l | u | o | h | s | g | u |
| r | a | b | s | t | r | n | o |
| e | f | b | t | h | s | i | y |
| t | r | i | r | p | e | w | s |
| a | i | s | t | h | a | t | g |
| w | t | h | i | r | s | t | y |
| t | n | d | l | u | o | h | s |

Unit 7

# Extension worksheet 2

**Pupil A – Ask your partner about the Zebra Swallowtail butterfly and write the answers. Then answer your partner's questions about the Red Admiral butterfly.**

## Zebra Swallowtail butterfly

| | |
|---|---|
| What colour? | |
| How big / wings? | |
| Where / live? | |
| Interesting fact? | |

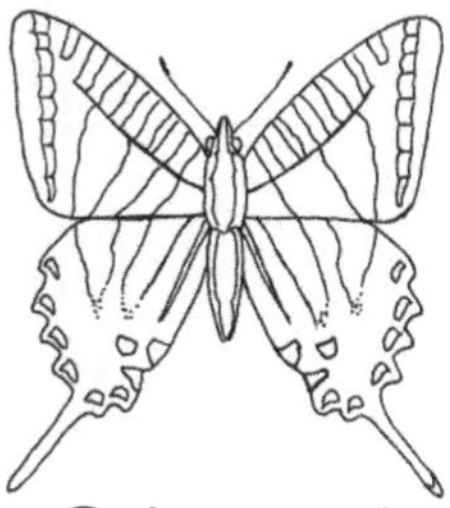

Colour me!

## Red Admiral butterfly

| | |
|---|---|
| What colour? | It's brown. It's got white spots and red stripes. |
| How big / wings? | They're 6 cm long. |
| Where / live? | They live in gardens and parks. |
| Interesting fact? | If they fly quickly in pairs, there is going to be a storm. |

**Pupil B – Answer your partner's questions about the Zebra Swallowtail butterfly. Then ask your partner about the Red Admiral butterfly and write the answers.**

## Zebra Swallowtail butterfly

| | |
|---|---|
| What colour? | It's got black and white stripes. It's got red and blue spots. |
| How big / wings? | They're 8 cm long. |
| Where / live? | They live near rivers. |
| Interesting fact? | It's got two long tails. Other animals think it's a bird. |

## Red Admiral butterfly

| | |
|---|---|
| What colour? | |
| How big / wings? | |
| Where / live? | |
| Interesting fact? | |

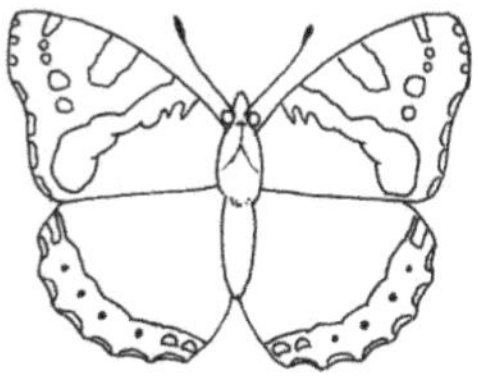

Colour me!

Unit 7

# Song worksheet

**1** (13) **Listen and think of actions for each line of the song.**

1 You shouldn't drop your rubbish,
2 You should put it in a bin.
3 You shouldn't leave it on the ground,
4 You should clean up everything.
5 Here comes the bear, here comes the bear!
6 It's coming for your tea!
7 Should I move or should I stop?
8 Should I climb that tree?
9 I should do something now.
10 That bear is after me.
11 You shouldn't go across the field,
12 You should walk around.
13 You shouldn't go too near that cow,
14 It can push you to the ground.
15 You should run, you should run,
16 You should jump quickly.
17 Should I move or should I stop?
18 Should I climb that tree?
19 I should do something now.
20 That cow is after me!

**2** (14) **Sing the song and do the actions.**

Unit 7

# Topic worksheet

## 1 Read about animal camouflage. Fill in the three titles.

**Pattern** **Smells and poison** **Colour**

Imagine you are a small creature. You have lots of enemies. People want to collect you. Animals want to eat or kill you. You cannot run quickly. So what should you do? Climb a tree? Run? No. You should hide – using camouflage. There are many types of camouflage:

**1** ..................................................

Many animals look like their natural home. Rabbits and other animals are brown, like the trees and the earth where they live. Many frogs are green, so they can hide in the green leaves. Polar bears have black skin but their white fur helps them to hide in the snow or ice. Some animals can change the colour of their fur or feathers in winter, autumn and summer.

**2** ..................................................

Different species have things on their fur, wings, tails or feathers so that their enemies cannot see them very well or are afraid of them. For example, some butterflies have two big spots on their wings. The spots look like eyes. Enemies think that they are snakes and stay away. The Indian Leaf butterfly has wings that look like dead leaves. Enemies think the butterflies are plants and so they don't try to catch them.

**3** ..................................................

Birds and insects can catch caterpillars very easily because the caterpillars can't move quickly. So they have to make themselves taste or smell bad. Some caterpillars make a bad smell. The enemy doesn't like it and goes away. If enemies eat some kinds of frogs and butterflies, they feel sick or can die.

## 2 Look at the pictures. What camouflage do these animals use?

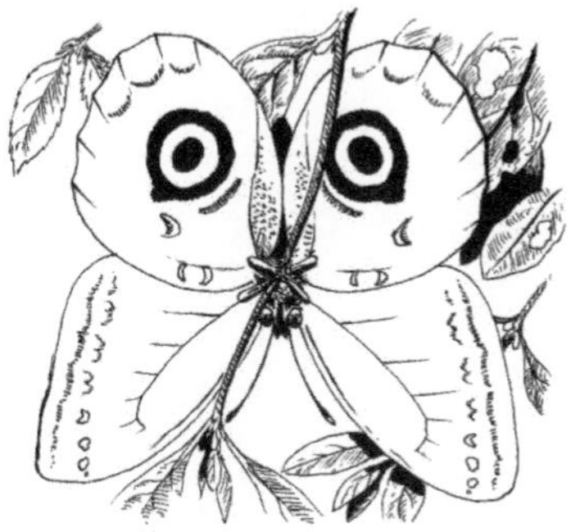

# 8 Teacher's notes

## Reinforcement worksheet 1

- Pupils complete the questions with the correct past participle and then answer the questions to see what prize they've won.

**Key:** visited, won, stopped, not done, cooked, climbed, sailed, been, painted.

- ***Optional follow-up activity:*** Pupils work in pairs and design a similar game. They write ten new questions, using *Have you ever …* and add five new 'prizes'. Then they play the game!

## Reinforcement worksheet 2

- Pupils use the code to find the first three letters of six sports and then write the full names of the sports. Then they fill in the gaps to complete which sport is done when.

**Key: 1)** 2 athletics, 3 sledging, 4 snowboarding, 5 skiing, 6 football. **2)** 2 football – autumn and winter, 3 skiing – winter, 4 athletics – spring and summer, 5 snowboarding and sledging – winter.

- ***Optional follow-up activity:*** Pupils use the code to write the first three letters of other words from Unit 8 for their partners to work out.

## Extension worksheet 1

- Pupils complete the questions with *Have you ever … ?* and the verb. Then they read answers a–f and decide which question goes with each answer. Finally, pupils match the sports pictures to the questions/answers.

**Key: 1)** 2 Have you ever cycled in the Tour de France? 3 Have you ever run an important race in winter? 4 Have you ever lost the ball? 5 Have you ever fallen through a hole in the ice? 6 Have you ever wanted to do a different sport? **2)** b 6, c 3, d 1, e 2, f 5. **3)** golf a4, cycling e2, ice skating f5, skiing d1, athletics c3, sledging b6.

- ***Optional follow-up activity:*** Write prompts on the board for several sports with appropriate collocating verbs such as: *go cycling, do athletics, go sledging, play hockey.* Pupils copy them in the first column of a grid of five columns. At the top of the second column, they write Me and tick or cross the sports they have and haven't done. Then they interview three pupils using *Have you ever … ?* questions and ticking or crossing under their names in the three remaining columns.

## Extension worksheet 2

F towards

- This activity mirrors the second part of the Speaking Test. Pupils have to describe what's happening in the different pictures in a story. Ask questions to elicit useful vocabulary and pre-teach words like: *hole, ice, stuck, blade.* Pupils prepare their answers. In class, pupils work in pairs and talk about the pictures. Remind them that they should give as much detail as possible.
- ***Optional follow-up activity:*** Pupils imagine they were there when it happened. They write an email in the past tense to a friend, describing the event.

## Song worksheet

- Pupils look at the pictures and fill in the missing words. Explain that sometimes *-ed* sounds like /t/ or /d/ (*walked, skied*) and sometimes *-ed* sounds like /ɪd/ (*snowboarded, needed*). Then pupils read the song and underline the verbs ending in *-ed*. Finally, they write the verbs in the correct pronunciation 'goal net' and listen to the song to check their answers.

**Key: 1)** See Pupil's Book, page 75. **2)** /ɪd/: skated, /d/ /t/: played, skied, climbed, sledged, raced.

- ***Optional follow-up activity:*** Ask pupils to look back through the unit in the Pupil's Book and find past tense verbs ending in *-ed*. Write a list of them on the board. Pupils form small teams. Draw two *-ed* 'goals' as on the worksheet. Say the words on the board one by one. Pupils write the word in the correct 'goal' according to how the *-ed* ending is pronounced. One point for each word in the correct net.

## Topic worksheet

- Ask students how they feel when they haven't eaten for a while (tired, no energy). Explain that a *calorie* is a way to measure how much energy you get from food. Tell them that they are going to read about an *Olympic swimmer* called *Michael Phelps* who needs lots of calories. Pupils read the text and underline the food words. They then tick the pictures of foods that are in the text. Finally, pupils work in pairs to answer the questions.

**Key: 1)** Food words – egg sandwiches, cheese, tomato, onions, two cups of coffee, an omelette, potatoes, bread with sugar, chocolate pancakes, a plate of pasta, ham and cheese sandwiches, drinks, pizza. **2)** Food he doesn't eat is: chicken, apples, ice cream, sausages, carrots. **3)** 1 2,000, 2 12,000, 3 because they use a lot of energy when they play sport.

- ***Optional follow-up activity:*** Pupils imagine they are a famous sportsperson. They write a short description of their sport, what they do every day and how much they eat. e.g. *My name's ____________. I'm a famous ____________. I've won ____________ gold medals and I've ____________. To play my sport, I need to be very fit. So every day I ____________. Also, I burn a lot of energy in my sport, so I need to eat a lot of calories. Every day I eat ____________ and I drink ____________.*

# Reinforcement worksheet 1

**Use the words in brackets to complete the '*Have you ever…*' questions. Then play the game with a partner! Which prize does your partner win?**

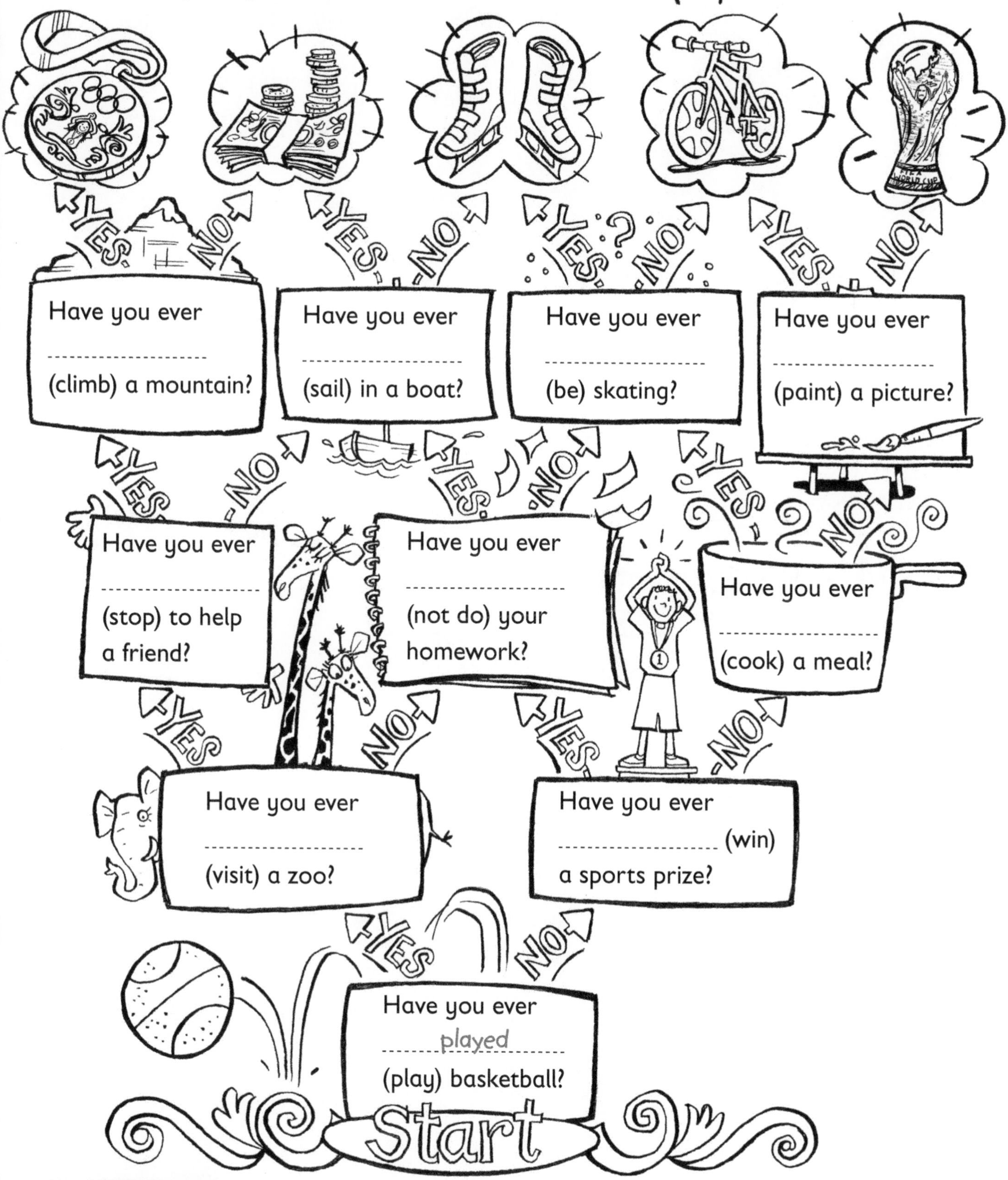
YES
NO
Have you ever ------------------- (climb) a mountain?
Have you ever ------------------- (sail) in a boat?
Have you ever ------------------- (be) skating?
Have you ever ------------------- (paint) a picture?
Have you ever ------------------- (stop) to help a friend?
Have you ever ------------------- (not do) your homework?
Have you ever ------------------- (cook) a meal?
Have you ever ------------------- (visit) a zoo?
Have you ever ------------------- (win) a sports prize?
Have you ever played (play) basketball?
Start

# Reinforcement worksheet 2

**1 Use the code to find the first three letters. Then write the names of the sports.**

1 8 – 15 – 3 hockey

2 1 – 20 – 8 ..............................

3 19 – 12 – 5 ..............................

4 19 – 14 – 15 ..............................

5 19 – 11 – 9 ..............................

6 6 – 15 – 15 ..............................

**2 Label the pictures. When do people usually do each sport?**

1 We usually play hockey in autumn and winter .

2 We usually play .................... in .................... and .................... .

3 We go .................... in .................... .

4 We usually do .................... in .................... and .................... .

 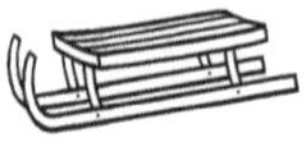 

5 We go .................... and .................... in .................... .

 Kid's Box BE Updated 2nd Ed. TRB 5 

Unit 8

# Extension worksheet 1

## 1 Complete these questions with *Have you ever* and the word in brackets.

1 Have you ever had (have) an accident on a mountain?

2 ........................ (cycle) in the Tour de France?

3 ........................ (run) an important race in winter?

4 ........................ (lose) the ball?

5 ........................ (fall) through a hole in the ice?

6 ........................ (want) to do a different sport?

## 2 Find the answers to questions 1–6.

a Yes. The balls I use are so small that they often get lost in trees or long grass. 4

b No, this sport is my favourite because you go very fast through the snow and it's safer than skiing. ..........

c Yes, but in winter we run inside so that it's not too cold. ..........

d Yes, I hurt my leg last winter on Mont Blanc. ..........

e No, but I want to ride my new racing bike in the next one. ..........

f No, because I don't do my sport on frozen lakes. I do it on special ice rinks. ..........

## 3 Decide which question and answer goes with each picture.

golf a4

cycling ☐

ice skating ☐

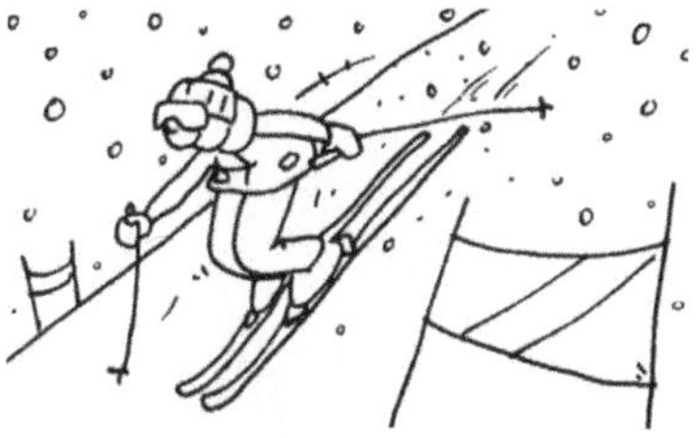

skiing ☐

athletics ☐

sledging ☐

  

Unit 8

# Extension worksheet 2

**Look at the pictures and think about the answers to the questions for each picture. Be ready to talk about the pictures.**

1 What's the weather like? What are the children going to do? Where?

2 What are the children doing? What are they wearing? How do they feel?

3 What's happened to the little boy? Where is his foot?

4 What are the older children trying to do? What's happening to the ice?

5 Why has the girl taken her skate off? How is the little boy feeling?

6 How is the little boy getting out of the water? How is he feeling now?

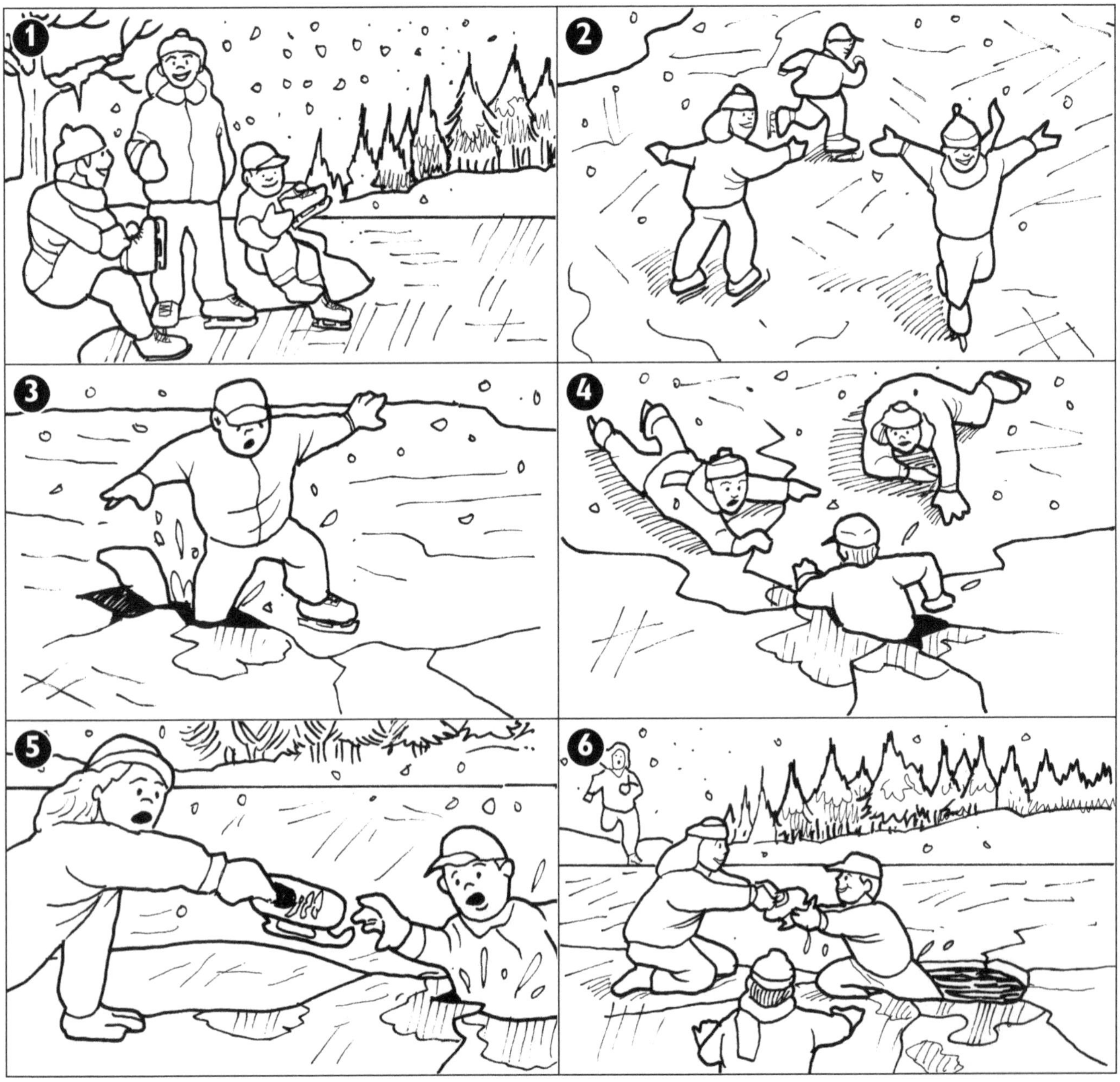

Unit 8

# Song worksheet

## 1 Look at the pictures and complete the song.

We love sport, swimming, sailing, running,

We love sport,

We love to do it all.

We've <u>skied</u> down a ___mountain___ ,

We've ________ up a rock,

We've played ________ with grandma,

We've raced against the ________ .

We've played ________ and tennis,

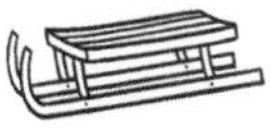

We've ________ in the snow,

We've skated in the ________ ,

We've made a ________ to throw.

Some like playing ___football___ ,

Some like watching it.

It's good to move your ________ ,

DON'T JUST SIT!

## 2 Look at the example. Underline the other *-ed* words in the song and put them in the goals.

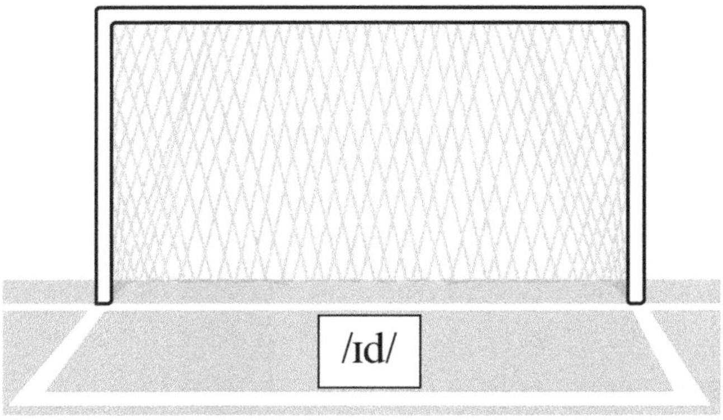


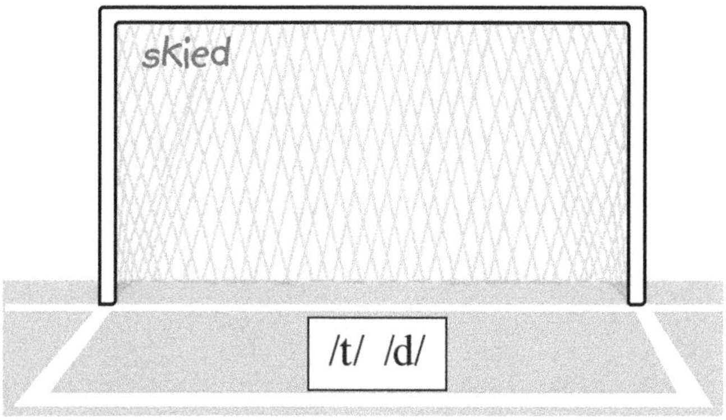


## 3 15 Listen and sing!

  

# Unit 8 Topic worksheet

**1 Michael Phelps is a famous Olympic swimmer. Underline all the foods he eats and drinks. Can you eat this much every day?**

**Most people only need about 2,000 calories every day, but Michael Phelps eats 12,000 calories a day. Every day!**

 ✓

Here is how Michael Phelps starts his day: three egg sandwiches topped with cheese, tomato, and onions. And that's before breakfast!

For breakfast, he has two cups of coffee, a five-egg omelette, a bowl of potatoes, three slices of bread with sugar on top and three chocolate pancakes.

This famous swimmer's lunch is: a big plate of pasta and two large ham and cheese sandwiches on white bread. The best Olympic athlete in the history of the Olympic Games then completes his meal by drinking about 1,000 calories of drinks.

Dinner is two more plates of pasta and a whole pizza, which he eats with another 1,000 calories of drinks.

 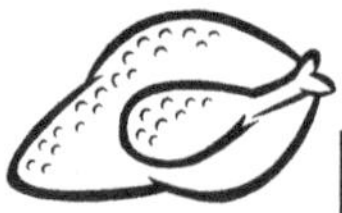  

**2 Tick (✓) the pictures of foods that Michael Phelps eats. What *doesn't* he eat?**

**3 Answer the questions:**

1. How many calories do most people need every day?
2. How many calories does Michael Phelps need every day?
3. Why do you think sports people need to eat so much?

# Festivals

## Christmas worksheet 1

- To ensure that pupils understand the activity, read through the instructions together and point out the first *job* word, *secretary*, which has been crossed out. Find one word in each of the other three categories. Pupils continue crossing out the words as instructed. Five words will be left (see key). To help pupils with this new vocabulary, they draw lines from the remaining five words to the pictures. Then pupils draw those five objects on the Christmas tree and colour it.

**Key:** Job words – manager, actor, fire fighter, teacher, dentist. Food words – biscuits, olives, cake, pizza. Sound like *snow* – throw, go, know, so. Five words from left to right – stars, stocking, candles, fairy, presents.

- ***Optional follow-up activity:*** Pupils make a Christmas card using their picture of a tree. They stick their picture onto the right-hand half of a piece of card. They fold the left-hand half behind the picture and write a Christmas message inside. (For example: *I hope you have a wonderful Christmas* or *Merry Christmas!*)

## Christmas worksheet 2

- Pupils read the jokes and talk about which ones they like best. Help them with useful vocabulary such as: *reindeer, Santa Claus, paws, Dracula* (the blood-sucking vampire), *ice caps*. Use the illustrations to help with this. Then they cut each joke out, taking care to follow the dotted lines. They put the eight slips of paper in a pile, one on top of the other. (Note: the blank slip should be on the top of the pile.) They staple the left-hand side of the pile. Pupils then design the cover on the top slip of paper. They can label it *My Christmas Joke Book* and colour it.
- ***Optional follow-up activity:*** Pupils make up some jokes of their own (or find more on the Internet). They can then write these jokes in their joke book (on the back of the existing jokes). If they write seven jokes, they could create a joke book that can be used in both directions – front to back, and back to front.

## Easter worksheet 1

- Explain that, in many countries, it is traditional for children to *hunt* for real or chocolate eggs on Easter Day. The Easter Bunny *hides* the eggs. Ask pupils to look at the picture and spot the Easter eggs (there are three) and the Easter Bunny. Elicit vocabulary for things they can see in the picture, e.g. *bridge, river, path*. Pupils write instructions for the two children (who are in the left-hand corner), telling them how to find the Easter eggs. Finally pupils colour the picture.

**Key: 1)** There are three Easter eggs. The Easter Bunny is behind the big tree. **2)** 1 Walk straight on. Turn left at the big tree. Walk along the river. There is a bridge on the left. Cross the bridge into the field of flowers. The egg is on the left, next to the bridge. 2 Walk straight on. Don't turn left or right when you see the big tree. Go straight on. There is a small house at the end of the path. The egg is under some trees on the right of the house. 3 Walk straight on. Turn right when you get to the big tree. Walk past the cave and go straight on. There is a small lake at the end of the path. The egg is across the lake. You can use the boat to get there!

- ***Optional follow-up activity:*** Pupils make an Easter card using their picture. They stick their picture onto the right-hand half of a piece of card. They fold the left-hand half behind the picture and write an Easter message inside (*Happy Easter!*)

## Easter worksheet 2

- Pupils read the jokes. You will need to help them with the word plays, particularly for *hairbrush, hairspray, exercise, aerobics, hot cross buns* (a bread-based cake with a cross on top, eaten hot with butter at Easter.), e.g. pronunciation of *harebrush* sounds the same as *hairbrush*, *harerobics* sounds nearly the same as *aerobics*. Pupils talk about which jokes they like best. Then they cut each joke out, taking care to follow the dotted lines. They put the eight slips of paper in a pile, one on top of the other. (Note: the blank slip should be on the top of the pile.) They staple the left-hand side of the pile. Pupils then design the cover on the top slip of paper. They can label it *My Easter Joke Book* and colour it.
- ***Optional follow-up activity:*** Pupils write the question and answer for each joke on separate equally-sized pieces of card and play Pelmanism with them. Refer to the rules of Pelmanism in the Optional follow-up activity for Unit 1, Extension worksheet 1.

# Christmas worksheet 1

**1 Look at the lists of words and follow the instructions.**

Cross out all the words which are jobs. The first one is done for you.
Cross out all the words which are types of food.
Cross out all the words which sound like *snow*.
Cross out the words *We wish you a Merry Christmas.*
What other five words about Christmas can you see?
Draw lines from the last five words to the pictures.

| | | | |
|---|---|---|---|
| ~~manager~~ | go | candles | you |
| We | stocking | cake | a |
| stars | wish | know | presents |
| throw | fire fighter | teacher | so |
| biscuits | Merry | fairy | pizza |
| actor | olives | Christmas | dentist |

**2 Now decorate the Christmas tree with pictures of the five Christmas words.**

# Christmas worksheet 2

**1 Read these Christmas jokes. Which ones do you like best?**

| | |
|---|---|
| What do snowmen wear on their heads? | *Ice caps!* |
| What did Dracula say at the Christmas party? | *Would you like a bite?* |
| What do snowmen eat for lunch? | *Icebergers!* |
| Who takes presents to cats at Christmas? | *Santa Paws!* |
| What's the best thing to put into a Christmas cake? | *Your teeth!* |
| What's the best thing to give your friends for Christmas? | *A list of everything you want!* |
| What do you call a reindeer with a fur hat? | *Anything you want – he can't hear you!* |

**2 Make your own joke book! First, cut round the edge of each joke. Next put the jokes in a pile. Then staple them together on the left and design the cover.**

# Easter worksheet 1

**1** **John and his sister Sue are looking for Easter eggs. How many Easter eggs can you see? Where is the Easter Bunny?**

**2** **Help John and Sue to find the Easter eggs. Complete the directions.**

1 Walk straight on. Turn left at the big tree. Walk along the river. There is a bridge on the left. Cross ..............................

2 ..............................

..............................

3 ..............................

..............................

**3** **Now colour the picture.**

# Easter worksheet 2

**1 Read these Easter jokes. Which ones do you like best?**

| | |
|---|---|
| Why isn't the Easter Bunny fat? | *Because he does lots of eggsercise!* |
| How does Easter end? | *With the letter R!* |
| What happens if you pour hot water on bunnies? | *You get hot cross bunnies!* |
| How does the Easter Bunny stay fit? | *He does lots of harerobics!* |
| How does the Easter Bunny keep his hair nice? | *With a harebrush!* |
| What do you call a rabbit that tells good jokes? | *A funny bunny!* |
| How does a rabbit keep his fur looking good? | *With harespray!* |

**2 Make your own joke book! First, cut round the edge of each joke. Next put the jokes in a pile. Then staple them together on the left and design the cover.**

# Test Units Welcome-2 Listening

**Name:** ...............................................

**Class:** ...............................................

**1** (16) **Listen and draw lines. There is one example.**

Harry Richard Alex Betty

Sarah Emma David

**2** **17** **Listen and write. There is one example.**

# CHANNEL 3
## needs TEENAGE ACTORS
## for a new television series!

| | | |
|---|---|---|
| | **Full name:** | Peter Clark |
| 1 | **Age:** | ................ |
| 2 | **Favourite TV series:** | ................ is Cool |
| 3 | **Favourite actor:** | Will ................ |
| 4 | **Day to visit Channel 3:** | ................ |
| 5 | **Time:** | ................ |

**3** **18** **What is each pupil's favourite school subject? Listen and write a letter in each box. There is one example.**

Katy ☐

Ben E

Mary ☐

Bill ☐

Emma ☐

Tom ☐

A

B

C

D

E

F

G

H

 

## 4 (19) Listen and tick (✓) the box. There is one example.

Where's Ben's mum going to work?

A ☑

B ☐

C ☐

**1** What job is Ben's mum going to do?

A ☐

B ☐

C ☐

**2** Who's Ben's mum going to work for?

A ☐

B ☐

C ☐

**3** When's Ben's mum going to start her new job?

A ☐

B ☐

C ☐

**4** What kind of TV programme is the School of Archaeology going to be in?

A ☐

B ☐

C ☐

**5** What's Ben's mum's job now?

A ☐

B ☐

C ☐

## 5 20 Listen and colour and write. There is one example.

# Test Units Welcome-2

**Reading and Writing**

**Name:** ....................................................

**Class:** ....................................

## 1 Look and read. Choose the correct words and write them on the lines. There is one example.

history | the news | ~~the weather~~ | a fire fighter | doctors | an ezine | a dictionary

a journalist | pilots | geography | cartoons | dentists | science | a notebook

On this programme, they tell you if it's going to be sunny, windy or rainy. ......the weather......

1 It's a kind of book. When we don't understand a word, we can use this. ..............................

2 These are TV programmes for children. They're 'moving pictures' and they're very funny. ..............................

3 This is a kind of job. When there is a fire, this person puts it out. ..............................

4 It's a school subject. In this lesson, we learn about plants and the human body. ..............................

5 These people wear a uniform. They fly aeroplanes. ..............................

6 If you like learning about the past, you should study this subject. ..............................

7 In this school subject, you can learn about different countries and people. ..............................

8 These people help you when you have a toothache. They clean your teeth too. ..............................

9 This is a kind of TV programme. You watch it when you want to know what is happening in the world. ..............................

10 This is something you read. It's a kind of internet magazine. Pupils write about interesting things in it. ..............................

**2** **Alvin is talking to his teacher, Mrs Hill. What does Mrs Hill say? Read the conversation and choose the best answer. Write a letter (A–H) for each answer. You do not need to use all the letters.**

*Example*

**Alvin:** Excuse me, Mrs Hill. Can I ask you some questions? It's for my ezine project.

**Mrs Hill:** ....C....

*Questions*

**1**

**Alvin:** You're an artist. Did you like art when you were at school?

**Mrs Hill:** ..........

**2**

**Alvin:** Where do you usually paint?

**Mrs Hill:** ..........

**3**

**Alvin:** Do you like painting animals?

**Mrs Hill:** ..........

**4**

**Alvin:** What are you going to paint next?

**Mrs Hill:** ..........

**5**

**Alvin:** Great. That's all. Thank you for your time, Mrs Hill.

**Mrs Hill:** ..........

**A** A picture for my husband's birthday.

**B** At home. I have a special room there.

**C** Of course. What would you like to know? (*Example*)

**D** You're welcome, Alvin. Good luck!

**E** At seven o'clock in the morning.

**F** Yes, I do. But I think people are more interesting.

**G** Yes, I did. It was my favourite subject.

**H** My husband's an artist too!

## 3 Read the story. Choose a word from the box. Write the correct word next to numbers 1–5. There is one example.

| |
|---|
| *example* |
| ~~School~~ quickly important happy library forty |
| run talk newspaper phone |

Yesterday Alvin and Shari were at Park Road ....School.... .

They wanted to watch TV, so they looked at a **(1)** .......................... .

A sports quiz was on television at four o'clock. Alvin and Shari love quizzes, but it was already three **(2)** .......................... !

So they started to run home **(3)** .......................... . But when they ran through the park, they saw a fire.

Shari stopped running. 'Come on!' Alvin said. 'We're late.'

He was angry because he didn't want to miss the quiz. But Shari knew that it was dangerous to leave the fire.

'No, Alvin. I'm going to **(4)** .......................... the fire fighters,' she said. Five minutes later the fire fighters arrived. 'Well done!' a fire fighter told them. 'You did the right thing.' Alvin felt good. He thought Shari was right. Putting out a fire was more **(5)** .......................... than a TV sports quiz.

**(6) Now choose the best name for the story.**
**Tick (✓) one box.**

The sports quiz ☐ A fire in the park ☐ Always leave a fire ☐

## 4 Read the text. Choose the right words and write them on the lines.

### Learn to spell well

*Example* Are you good at learning to ...write... new words in your first language
1 or a second language? .............. you know if *science* or *sceince* is the correct spelling in English? (It's *science*, of course.)

2 .............. you are learning a second language it is sometimes difficult to learn to spell new words, and to remember the correct spelling. But
3 .............. are lots of things you can do to make this easier.

One very important thing is to buy a good dictionary or find an online
4 dictionary that you like .............. . You can also have a notebook
5 where you write down .............. new word you learn. Another good
6 idea is to stick new words .............. a wall in your house so you see the
7 words each day. You .............. also read lots of the books you enjoy, so you see lots of different words without having to work very hard.

8 Some schools have spelling competitions. They are .............. 'Spelling Bees', where the student who can spell the most words without any
9 mistakes .............. a prize. These competitions help children learn lots
10 of new words. .............. don't you have one in your English class?

| | | | |
|---|---|---|---|
| ***Example*** | writing | write | writes |
| 1 | Are | Do | Can |
| 2 | So | But | When |
| 3 | they | there | those |
| 4 | using | use | used |
| 5 | all | many | every |
| 6 | on | in | at |
| 7 | shall | will | should |
| 8 | call | calling | called |
| 9 | win | winning | wins |
| 10 | How | Why | Where |

 

## 5 Look at the picture and read the story. Write some words to complete the sentences about the story. You can use 1, 2, 3 or 4 words.

### The music competition

Harry's favourite subject at school is music. He has music classes on Monday and Friday. He loves them. At home, he likes playing the guitar and singing too. 'You're going to be a great singer one day,' his music teacher often tells him.

One day Harry's music teacher told him about a music competition. 'In September there's going to be a very important competition with a big prize,' she said. Harry was really interested. 'I think you should sing in the competition,' she told him. 'But first you are going to need a lot of practice,' she said. 'Come to school early every morning and we can practise your songs before the other pupils arrive.'

The next week Harry had to wake up at 6:00 every morning and leave the house at 6:30 to walk to school. He practised singing with his music teacher, but he was really tired. Harry didn't like getting up early! And it was a lot of work. 'Can you repeat that song, Harry?' she asked again and again.

At the competition he sang very well. But when he won the second prize, he was sad. 'You said I'm going to be a great singer, but I didn't win,' he told his teacher. 'Harry, you did very well but if you want to be a great singer, you have to work harder than all the other singers in the world,' she said.

***Examples***

Music is Harry's favourite subject at school.

He enjoys singing and playing the guitar .

***Questions***

1 Harry's music classes are on ______________ each week.

2 Harry's teacher thinks that one day Harry can be a ______________ .

3 The competition was in the month of ______________ .

4 Every morning of the next week Harry woke up at ______________ o'clock.

5 Harry walked to ______________ to practise with his music teacher.

6 He sang very ______________ at the competition.

7 At the competition he won the ______________ .

**6** **Read the diary and write the missing words. Write one word on each line.**

Sunday

| | |
|---|---|
| ***Example*** | This afternoon, I ......went...... to John's house with Jen. We |
| **1** | arrived at quarter to four because we wanted to .................. the cartoons on TV at four o'clock. But when we turned on the television, a sports programme was on. 'Oh no!' I hate golf!' said Jen. We tried the other channels but there were no cartoons on any of them. 'What can we do now?' I |
| **2** | .................. John and Jen. Before they could answer, John's mum came into the room. |
| **3** | She .................. a great idea. 'Why don't you *make* a cartoon?' she said. |
| **4** | She is .................. artist and she showed us how to do it. |
| **5** | So we all made a cartoon. We drew lots .................. pictures. It was a really amazing afternoon! |

**7** **Look at the three pictures. Write about this story. Write 20 or more words.**

--------------------------------------------------------------------------------

--------------------------------------------------------------------------------

--------------------------------------------------------------------------------

--------------------------------------------------------------------------------

# Test Units Welcome-2

**Speaking**

1

Teacher's card

**Find the Differences**

Pupil's card

**Find the Differences**

## 2

Teacher's card

**Nick**

| | |
|---|---|
| How / old / Nick | ? |
| Documentaries interesting / boring | ? |
| Hobbies | ? |
| How many brothers and sisters | ? |
| Going to be | ? |

**Jenny**

| | |
|---|---|
| How / old / Jenny | 12 |
| Documentaries interesting / boring | interesting |
| Hobbies | playing football, swimming |
| How many brothers and sisters | three |
| Going to be | a scientist |

**Find Information. Ask and answer.**

Pupil's card

**Nick**

| | |
|---|---|
| How / old / Nick | 13 |
| Documentaries interesting / boring | boring |
| Hobbies | playing the guitar, singing |
| How many brothers and sisters | two |
| Going to be | a computer science teacher |

**Jenny**

| | |
|---|---|
| How / old / Jenny | ? |
| Documentaries interesting / boring | ? |
| Hobbies | ? |
| How many brothers and sisters | ? |
| Going to be | ? |

**Find Information. Ask and answer.**

# 3 The science test

Tuesday

Tuesday

Wednesday

Michael

Thursday

Friday

## Tell the Story

# Test Units 3–4



**Name:** ..............................................................

**Class:** ..............................................

**1** 21 **Listen and draw lines. There is one example.**

Anna Kim Helen Robert

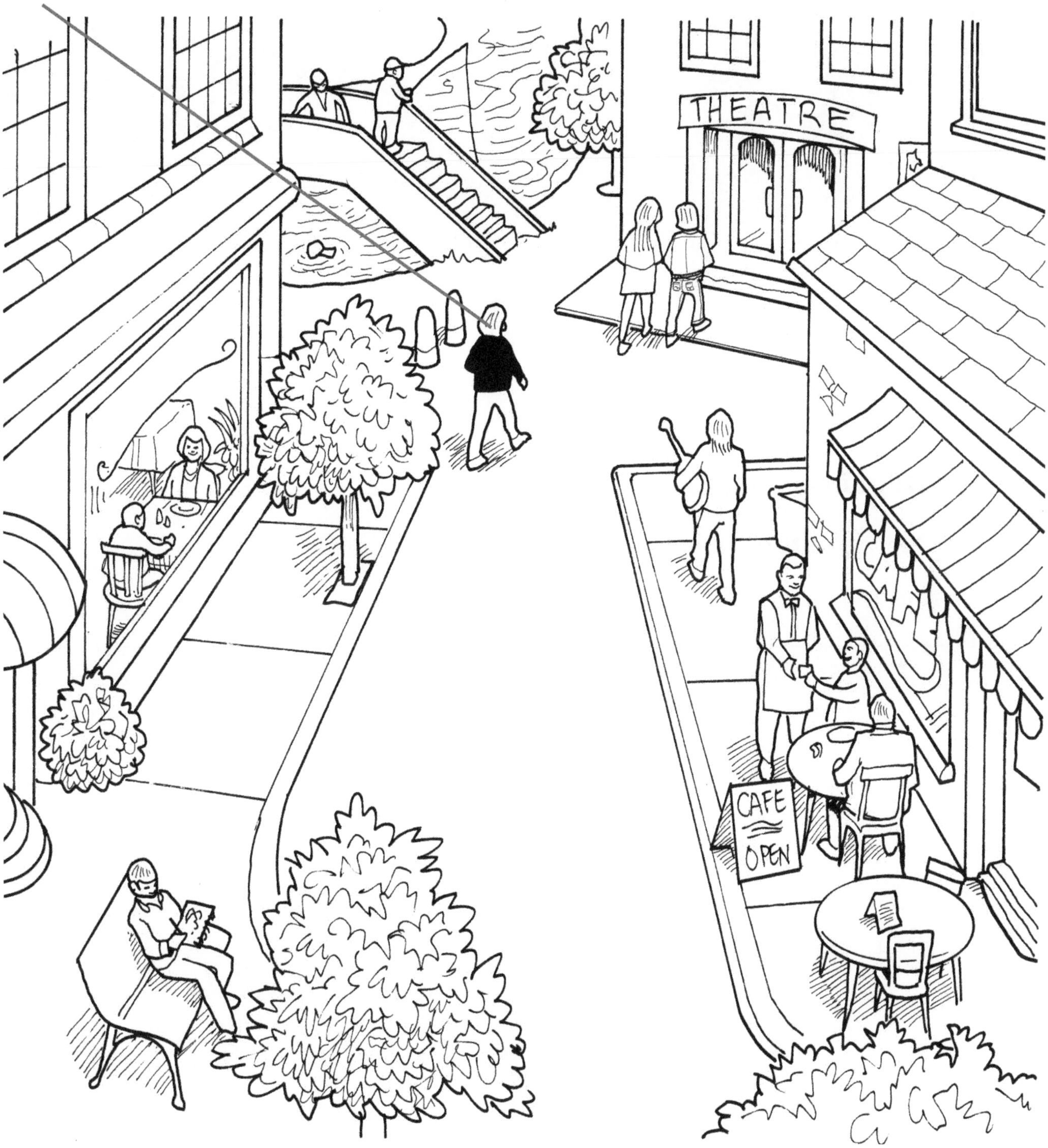


Bill Michael Jack

 

**2** 22 **Listen and write. There is one example.**

## Welcome to London!

| | | |
|---|---|---|
| | **Name:** | Sarah Perez |
| 1 | **Age:** | ........................ |
| 2 | **Staying at:** | The ........................ Hotel |
| 3 | **In London with:** | ........................ |
| 4 | **Days in London:** | Monday to ........................ |
| 5 | **Name of toy shop:** | ........................ |

 

**3** **23** **What happened to the pupils in Robert's class? Listen and write a letter in each box. There is one example.**

Mary ☐

Vicky [F]

Alex ☐

Jane ☐

William ☐

David ☐

A

B

C

D

E

F

G

H

  

## 4 (24) Listen and tick (✓) the box. There is one example.

Where in town was the fire?

A ✓

B ☐

C ☐

1 Where was the café?

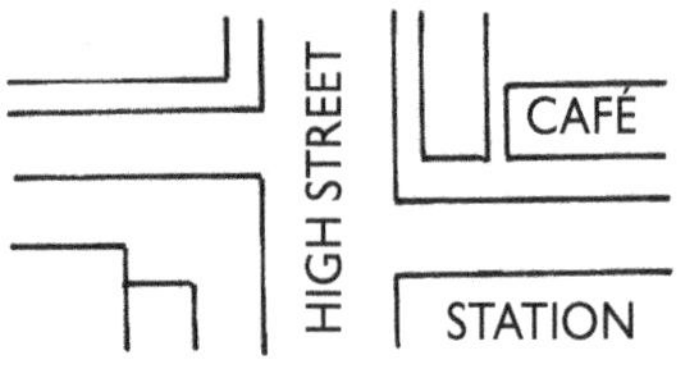


A ☐

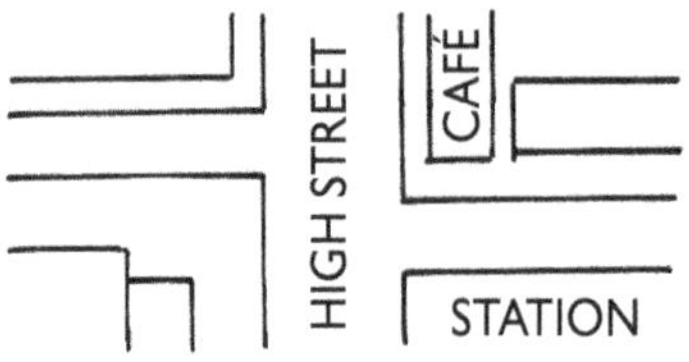


B ☐

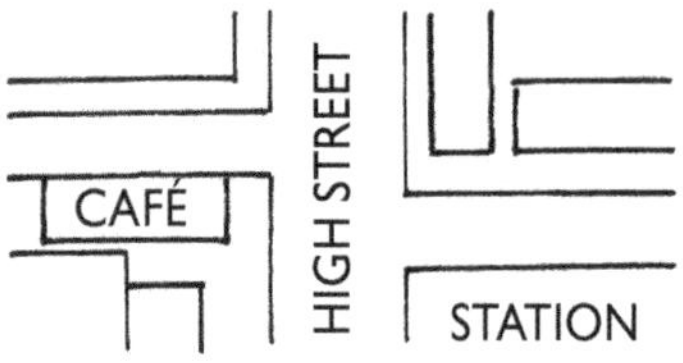


C ☐

2 Where did the fire start?

A ☐

B ☐

C ☐

3 What was Mr Green doing when the fire started?

A ☐

B ☐

C ☐

4 What did the customers do when the fire started?

A ☐

B ☐

C ☐

5 Where did the man hear about the fire?

A ☐

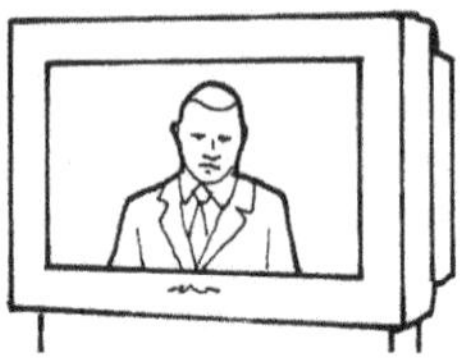

B ☐

C ☐

5 25 **Listen and colour and write. There is one example.**

# Test Units 3–4

**Reading and Writing**

**Name:** ..............................................................

**Class:** ..............................................

**1** **Look and read. Choose the correct words and write them on the lines. There is one example.**

fire stations    December    July

a castle    an airport    February    museums    hotels

October    a factory    a bridge    a bank    a stadium

~~a skyscraper~~    January

This is a very tall building with lots of floors. a skyscraper

1 If you want to cross a river, you walk over this. ..............................

2 It's a really strong building. The Queen lives in one. ..............................

3 This is a month. It's the one after September. ..............................

4 People don't live in these buildings. Fire fighters work in them. ..............................

5 Christmas is in this month. It's the last month of the year. ..............................

6 These buildings have lots of interesting things to see. The 'Rosetta Stone' is in one. ..............................

7 This month is between June and August. ..............................

8 This is a place where you can catch a plane. ..............................

9 In this place in town you can get money. ..............................

10 This is the shortest month in the year. In most years it's only got 28 days. ..............................

**2** **Luke is at the zoo, but he can't find the penguins. He asks a zoo keeper, Rachel, for help. What does Rachel say?**
**Read the conversation and choose the best answer.**
**Write a letter (A–H) for each answer.**
**You do not need to use all the letters.**

***Example***

**Luke:** Excuse me. Can you help me?

**Rachel:** ....C....

***Questions***

**1**

**Luke:** Are there any penguins here, please?

**Rachel:** ..........

**2**

**Luke:** Can you tell me where the penguins are?

**Rachel:** ..........

**3**

**Luke:** What do penguins like to eat?

**Rachel:** ..........

**4**

**Luke:** Where can I buy some food for the penguins?

**Rachel:** ..........

**5**

**Luke:** I'm going to get some for the penguins' dinner.

**Rachel:** ..........

**A** Fish. They swim really fast and catch them in the water.

**B** I love them too.

**C** Yes, of course. (***Example***)

**D** I'll show you on the map – go along this path and turn left at the big tree.

**E** The fruit shop? Take the third street on the right.

**F** Not here at the zoo. Maybe from the market.

**G** But you can't feed the animals in the zoo!

**H** Yes, the zoo has a great penguin area with a large pool.

**3** **Read the story. Choose a word from the box. Write the correct word next to numbers 1–5. There is one example.**

| *example* | | | | | | |
|---|---|---|---|---|---|---|
| ~~dad~~ | minutes | fall | most | paintings | across | more |
| corner | feel | bridge | | | | |

Last July, Sarah went on holiday with her mum and ........*dad*........ . On the first morning, they went to an art museum to look at some **(1)** .............................. . They walked for hours. At one o'clock, they were tired and hungry. So they decided to go and eat something.

There was a restaurant **(2)** .............................. the street, where Sarah ate a big pizza and drank some tea.

After lunch, they visited an old castle. It was one of the **(3)** .............................. beautiful castles in the country, on a hill above the river. Sarah and her parents loved it.

But when they were leaving, the ground suddenly started to move. It moved for about two **(4)** .............................. and then it stopped. 'What was that?' Dad asked. 'I think it was an earthquake!' said Mum. 'Don't worry,' said Dad. 'The buildings aren't going to **(5)** .............................. down.' He was right. It was only a very small earthquake, but Sarah had some exciting news to tell her friends when she got home.

(6) **Now choose the best name for the story. Tick (✓) one box.**

An exciting story ☐ Sarah's mum ☐ The castle on the hill ☐

## 4 Read the text. Choose the right words and write them on the lines.

### The Titanic

***Example*** The Titanic ___was___ the name of a very big ship.

**1** In 1912 ________ famous ship had a terrible disaster. It was
**2** ________ across the Atlantic Ocean from England to the USA
**3** ________ 14 April when it hit an iceberg. No one saw the iceberg
**4** because ________ was a lot of fog. Many people were having
**5** dinner in the restaurant ________ sleeping when the water
**6** ________ into the ship. Emily Haisman was only 15 years old.
**7** She was safe. With many women and children she climbed ________
**8** small boats and ________ on the sea for help.
**9** But ________ father and hundreds of other people died when
**10** the ship sank. It was the ________ ship disaster in history.

| | | | |
|---|---|---|---|
| ***Example*** | were | was | had |
| **1** | these | this | those |
| **2** | sailed | sail | sailing |
| **3** | on | by | at |
| **4** | it | there | they |
| **5** | or | when | but |
| **6** | coming | came | comes |
| **7** | under | into | through |
| **8** | waits | wait | waited |
| **9** | his | her | hers |
| **10** | worst | worse | bad |

**5** **Look at the picture and read the story. Write some words to complete the sentences about the story. You can use 1, 2, 3 or 4 words.**

## The school visit

On Tuesday 4 May, the science teacher, Mrs Wood, took the class to visit a science museum. It was an interesting museum, but Martin and his friends didn't like it. 'This is boring,' said Martin. When the science teacher wasn't looking, Martin and three friends ran to the park.

They played in the park for half an hour, but then they were bored again. It was only 11 o'clock. So they went to the river. 'This is fun!' said Martin. But when he was playing by the water, he fell in. The river was moving very quickly and he couldn't swim very well.

'Let's go and get the teacher,' said Martin's friends. So they ran to the museum and found her. 'Mrs Wood! Please come quickly! Martin is in the river!'

The teacher ran to the river. She could swim very well, so she jumped in and helped Martin.

Martin was feeling terrible when he climbed out of the river. He was wet, cold and sad. He said 'I'm sorry, Mrs Wood. I was very naughty.'

In June the class went to the city to visit the castle. This time Martin was good. He stayed next to the history teacher all the time.

### *Examples*

..........Tuesday 4 May.......... was the date that the class went to the science museum with Mrs Wood.

Martin thought that the science museum was ..........boring.......... and he didn't like it.

### *Questions*

1 Martin went with .............................. to the park.

2 At the park, they were bored after they played for .............................. .

3 They left the park at .............................. in the morning.

4 Martin .............................. the river when he was playing near it.

5 It was difficult for Martin to .............................. .

6 Martin felt .............................. when he came out of the water.

7 Martin's class went to a castle in the month of .............................. .

**6** **Read the letter and write the missing words. Write one word on each line.**

Dear Kate,

***Example*** How are you? I hope you ......are...... well. I'm fine. We are

**1** .................... holiday! I'm visiting interesting places in the city. It's

**2** really fun. But yesterday I .................... a terrible day! I was trying

to get to the museum and I got lost. The first person told me it was

**3** two streets past the park. The .................... person told me it was

on the corner of 6th Street and 24th Street. The third person told

**4** me it was next .................... the fire station. Finally, I got so tired

that I went home!

**5** Can you .................... me where the museum is?

Love,

Jane

**7** **Look at the three pictures. Write about this story. Write 20 or more words.**

------------------------------------------------------------

------------------------------------------------------------

------------------------------------------------------------

------------------------------------------------------------

1

Teacher's card

**Find the Differences**

Pupil's card

**Find the Differences**

2

Teacher's card

**Mary**

| | |
|---|---|
| Where / go / this morning | ? |
| Who / see | ? |
| What / Queen / say | ? |
| What time / Mary / leave | ? |
| What / do / this afternoon | ? |

**Richard**

| | |
|---|---|
| Where / go / this morning | fire station |
| Who / see | his uncle |
| What / uncle / say | 'I'm going to show you my work.' |
| What time / Richard / leave | 1:55 |
| What / do / this afternoon | play football in park |

**Find Information. Ask and answer.**

Pupil's card

**Mary**

| | |
|---|---|
| Where / go / this morning | castle |
| Who / see | Queen |
| What / Queen / say | 'Would you like some tea?' |
| What time / Mary / leave | 11:50 |
| What / do / this afternoon | go to museum |

**Richard**

| | |
|---|---|
| Where / go / this morning | ? |
| Who / see | ? |
| What / uncle / say | ? |
| What time / Richard / leave | ? |
| What / do / this afternoon | ? |

**Find Information. Ask and answer.**

 

# 3 Fred loses his dog

## Tell the Story

# Test Units 5–6

Listening

**Name:** ................................................

**Class:** ................................................

**1** 26 **Listen and draw lines. There is one example.**

Mary Sarah Harry Fred

Lucy Jim Alex

## 2 27 Listen and write. There is one example.

# Katy's Party

| | | |
|---|---|---|
| | **Name:** | Katy Barker |
| 1 | **Having a party at:** | ........................ |
| 2 | **Giving money to:** | 'Help the ........................' |
| 3 | **Katy's food:** | chocolate ........................ |
| 4 | **Number of people:** | ........................ |
| 5 | **Telephone number:** | ........................ |

**3** **28** **What did the children in the class make? Listen and write a letter in each box. There is one example.**

Anna [D]

David [ ]

John [ ]

Sally [ ]

Katy [ ]

Richard [ ]

A

B

C

D

E

F

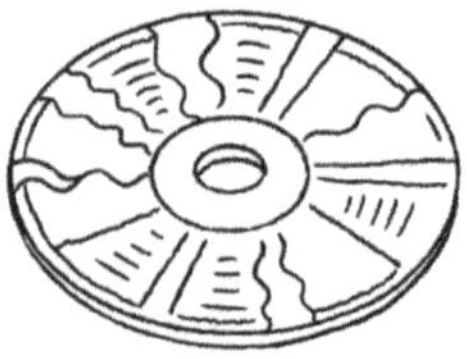

G

H

 

## 4 Listen and tick (✓) the box. There is one example.

Where was Jason's birthday party?

A ☐

B ☑

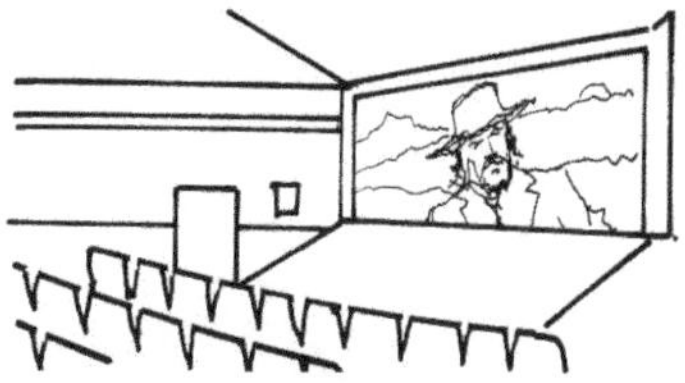

C ☐

1 Why didn't Grandma go to the birthday party?

A ☐

B ☐

C ☐

2 What did Jason eat?

A ☐

B ☐

C ☐

3 What did the birthday cake look like?

A ☐

B ☐

C ☐

4 What was Jason's favourite present?

A ☐

B ☐

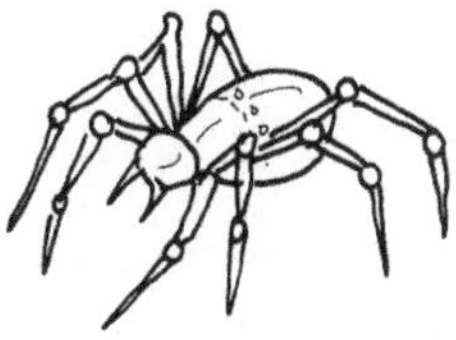

C ☐

5 When is Jason going to visit his grandparents?

A ☐

B ☐

C ☐

5 30 **Listen and colour and write. There is one example.**

# Test Units 5–6

**Reading and Writing**

**Name:** ..................................................

**Class:** ..................................................

**1 Look and read. Choose the correct words and write them on the lines. There is one example.**

| | | | |
|---|---|---|---|
| paper | a costume | meals | |
| a bowl | a scarf | salt | spoons |
| a knife | ~~plastic~~ | pepper | wood |
| fur | glass | plates | gold |

This material is made using oil. Cameras, bags and computers are often made of it. ......plastic......

1 They're round. You put pizza and other food on them. ..............................

2 We eat three of these every day. The first one is breakfast. The last one is dinner. ..............................

3 This is a kind of material. It's very warm and it comes from animals. Hats are often made of it. ..............................

4 This material is made from trees. We write on it. There is lots of it in your notebook. ..............................

5 This material can break easily. Bottles are usually made of it. ..............................

6 This makes food taste good. When you are cooking pasta, you put it into the water. ..............................

7 This is a kind of metal. It's expensive. Watches are sometimes made of it. ..............................

8 It's made of metal. You use it to cut bread and fruit. ..............................

9 It's made of wool and you wear it when it's cold. You put it around your neck. ..............................

10 These are often made of metal. You use them to eat soup and ice cream. ..............................

**2 Anne is bringing some materials to Mr Green to be recycled.**
**What does Anne say?**
**Read the conversation and choose the best answer.**
**Write a letter (A–H) for each answer.**
**You do not need to use all the letters.**

*Example*

**Mr Green:** Can I help you, Anne?

**Anne:** ....C....

*Questions*

**1**

**Mr Green:** What do you want to recycle?

**Anne:** ..........

**2**

**Mr Green:** Put the plastic bottles in the blue bin.

**Anne:** ..........

**3**

**Mr Green:** The bin on the left is full.

**Anne:** ..........

**4**

**Mr Green:** Have you got any clothes to recycle?

**Anne:** ..........

**5**

**Mr Green:** It's really good that you recycle things, Anne. Well done.

**Anne:** ..........

**A** What about the wood?

**B** Oh yes, I'll have to use the one on the right.

**C** Yes, please. I want to recycle some things. (***Example***)

**D** No, I haven't. That's everything for today, Mr Green.

**E** Some plastic bottles and some old newspapers.

**F** They're made of wool.

**G** OK. And I know the newspapers go in the red bins.

**H** Thank you. I think it's important.

## 3 Read the story. Choose a word from the box. Write the correct word next to numbers 1–5. There is one example.

| *example* | | | | | | |
|---|---|---|---|---|---|---|
| ~~mum~~ | taste | hungry | soft | sound | feel | look |
| terrible | cold | old | | | | |

Beth was staying with her grandparents when her ..........mum.......... called her. 'I've got a surprise for you. Guess what it is!' her mum said.

Beth and her mum often played this game. They asked questions about the five senses of smell, hearing, sight, touch and **(1)** .......................... .

Beth said, 'OK. First question: What does it **(2)** .......................... like? Is it pretty?' Mum said, 'Yes. It's small and beautiful.' Beth asked, 'Is it a toy?' Mum said, 'No. But you *can* play with it.'

'OK. What does it feel like?' Beth asked. Mum said, 'It feels **(3)** .......................... and warm.'

Beth asked, 'What does it taste like? Is it a cake?' Mum said, 'You can't *eat* it!' Then Beth said, 'I know! It's a cat!' Her mum said, 'No, but it is a kind of animal.'

Then Beth asked, 'What does it **(4)** .......................... like?' Mum said, 'Well, sometimes it's quiet and sometimes it's very noisy.' 'Is it a dog?' Beth asked but she was wrong again.

'OK. Fifth sense, Mum,' said Beth. 'What does it smell like?'

Mum said, 'Well, sometimes it smells nice and sometimes it smells **(5)** .......................... !'

'I know,' said Beth. 'It's a new baby!'

Mum said, 'Yes, it's your new baby sister! And she's two days old!'

**(6) Now choose the best name for the story.**
**Tick (✓) one box.**

A new person in the family ☐ Beth's new cat ☐ Something good to eat ☐

## 4 Read the text. Choose the right words and write them on the lines.

### Banana bread recipe

| | |
|---|---|
| ***Example*** | Many people all over the world like to ......eat...... bread. |
| **1** | Bread is a very healthy food .................... it gives people energy |
| **2** | .................... work, play or study. |
| **3** | It's easy to .................... delicious banana bread. |
| **4** | First, .................... mix the butter and sugar in a big bowl. Then |
| **5** | you add .................... egg and some mashed bananas. Next, |
| **6** | .................... another bowl, mix flour, baking soda and salt. |
| **7** | After that, mix the dry ingredients .................... the wet ones. |
| **8** | Put the banana bread in the oven and bake it for .................... hour. |
| **9** | Finally, .................... the banana bread out of the oven and cut it |
| **10** | into slices to eat with .................... friends. |

| | | | |
|---|---|---|---|
| ***Example*** | eats | eating | eat |
| **1** | because | if | but |
| **2** | and | to | or |
| **3** | made | makes | make |
| **4** | it | you | he |
| **5** | an | a | any |
| **6** | between | over | in |
| **7** | with | at | behind |
| **8** | one | two | some |
| **9** | took | take | taking |
| **10** | our | my | your |

 

## 5 Look at the picture and read the story. Write some words to complete the sentences about the story. You can use 1, 2, 3 or 4 words.

### The elephant

One day, Maria's teacher, Mrs White, came to class with some great news. 'The museum is having a competition! Every class is going to make an animal out of recycled materials,' she said. Maria and the other children were excited.

The children brought materials from home. Soon, the class had 50 paper cups, 6 boxes of newspapers, 2 paper plates and 2 plastic knives. 'What sort of animal are we going to make with these things?' asked the children. Mrs White smiled and said, 'Think of different animals and how you can make them!'

The children made a large space in the centre of the room and began to work. First, they made five very long things out of paper cups. Next, they made a large ball and a small ball out of newspaper.

Finally, they made the animal. The four long legs and a long nose, called a trunk, were made of the paper cups. The head and body were made from painted newspapers. The two ears were made of paper plates. The two long teeth, called tusks, were made of plastic knives. It was a beautiful elephant!

### *Examples*

Mrs White is Maria's ..........teacher.......... .

Mrs White had ....some great news.... for Maria and her classmates.

### *Questions*

1 There was a competition at the .............................. .

2 Children had to make .............................. from recycled materials for the competition.

3 The children felt .............................. about the competition.

4 The children used all kinds of .............................. that they got from home.

5 They had .............................. of newspapers.

6 The elephant's legs were made of the .............................. .

7 The children used .............................. to make the elephant's tusks.

## 6 Read the letter and write the missing words. Write one word on each line.

| | |
|---|---|
| ***Example*** | ......Dear...... Lucy, |
| **1** | Yesterday was my birthday .................... my family and I went to a restaurant to have pizza. |
| **2** | I watched the cook make the pizza .................... the kitchen. |
| **3** | First, she .................... the dough out of flour and water. |
| **4** | Then she threw .................... in the air to make it round. |
| | Next, she put tomato on the pizza. |
| | After that she added the cheese, mushrooms and olives. |
| **5** | It .................... delicious! |
| | Love, |
| | Mike |

## 7 Look at the three pictures. Write about this story. Write 20 or more words.

# Test Units 5–6

Speaking

1

Teacher's card

**Find the Differences**

Pupil's card

**Find the Differences**

 

**2**

Teacher's card

**John**

| | |
|---|---|
| What / making | ? |
| What / made of | ? |
| What / do first | ? |
| How long / take to make | ? |
| What / taste like | ? |

**Katy**

| | |
|---|---|
| What / making | soup |
| What / made of | water, 3 carrots and 4 onions |
| What / do first | cut the vegetables with a knife |
| How long / take to make | half an hour |
| What / taste like | very good |

**Find Information. Ask and answer.**

Pupil's card

**John**

| | |
|---|---|
| What / making | a sandwich |
| What / made of | bread, mayonnaise and 3 tomatoes |
| What / do first | spread mayonnaise on the bread |
| How long / take to make | 10 minutes |
| What / taste like | great |

**Katy**

| | |
|---|---|
| What / making | ? |
| What / made of | ? |
| What / do first | ? |
| How long / take to make | ? |
| What / taste like | ? |

**Find Information. Ask and answer.**

# 3 A birthday surprise

Daisy Betty

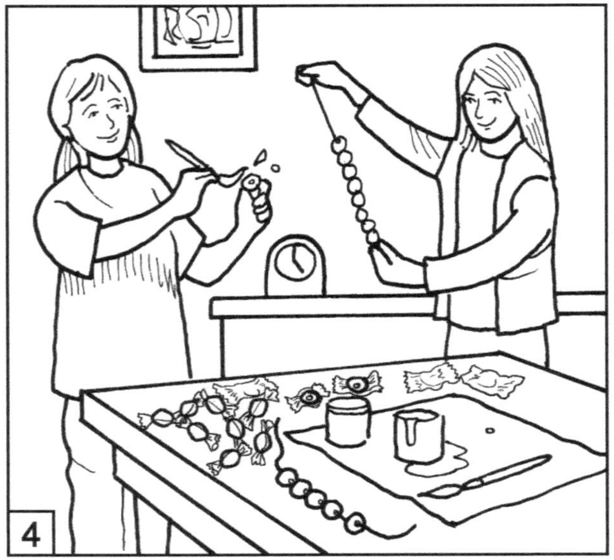


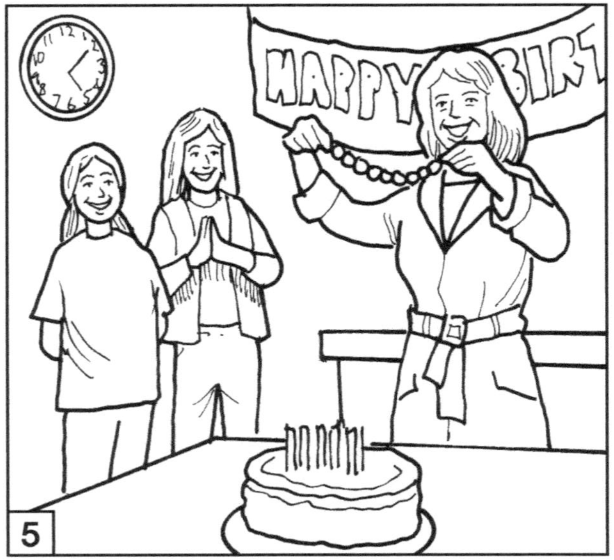


**Tell the Story**

 

# Test Units 7–8

Listening

**Name:** ..............................................................................

**Class:** ..................................................

**1** 31 **Listen and draw lines. There is one example.**

Jack Alex Daisy Betty

Paul William Jane

**2** 32 **Listen and write. There is one example.**

## Library Card

| | | |
|---|---|---|
| | **Name:** | David Richards |
| 1 | **Age:** | ............ |
| 2 | **School:** | ............ Road School |
| 3 | **Favourite subject:** | ............ |
| 4 | **Number of books every month:** | ............ |
| 5 | **Topic of ezine project:** | Tree ............ |

## 3 (33) What sports are the children good at?
## Listen and write a letter in each box. There is one example.

Anna [ ]

Nick [F]

John [ ]

Katy [ ]

Michael [ ]

Lucy [ ]

A

B

C

D

E

F

G

H

## 4 (34) Listen and tick (✓) the box. There is one example.

Which museum did Sarah go to?

A ☐

B ☑

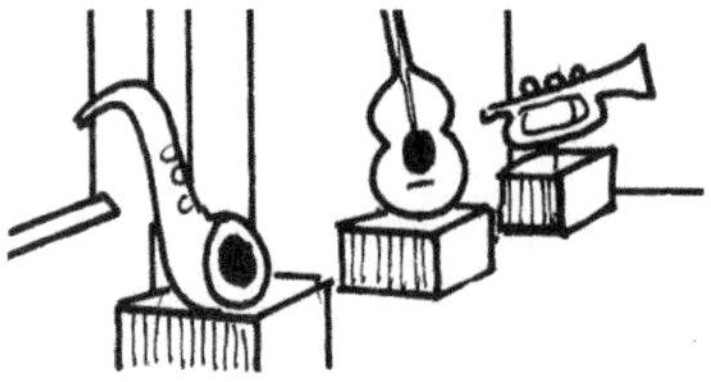

C ☐

1 How did Sarah travel to the museum?

A ☐

B ☐

C ☐

2 How long did it take to get to the museum?

30 MINUTES

A ☐

1 HOUR

B ☐

1 HOUR 30 MINUTES

C ☐

3 What did Sarah see at the museum?

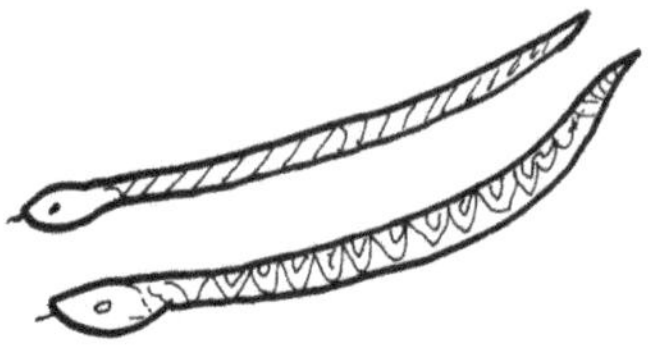

A ☐

B ☐

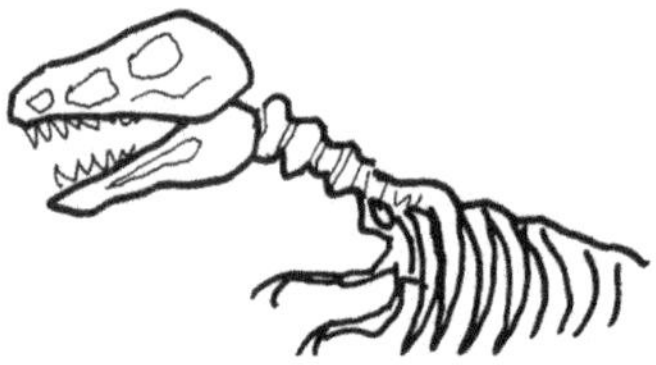

C ☐

4 Why did Sarah fall?

A ☐

B ☐

C ☐

5 What did the museum send to Sarah?

A ☐

B ☐

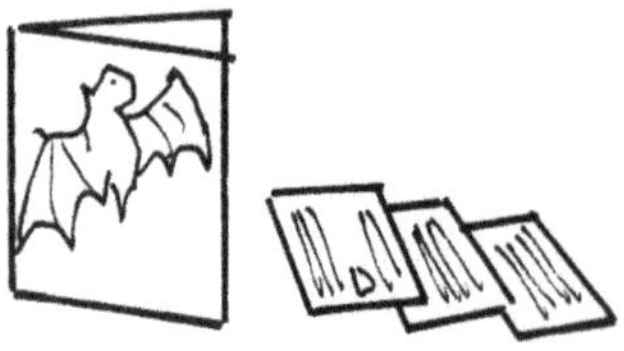

C ☐

## 5 35 Listen and colour and write. There is one example.

# Test Units 7–8

**Reading and Writing**

**Name:** ..............................................................................

**Class:** .................................................

**1** **Look and read. Choose the correct words and write them on the lines. There is one example.**

picnics striped extinct engines athletics endangered species rubbish butterflies summer spring ~~skiing~~ bottles eagles spots sledging

This is a sport which you do in the winter. You stand up and go downhill in the snow. ..........*skiing*..........

1. Some creatures have these on their bodies. They are round. ..............................
2. When the weather is nice, people have these. They eat them outside, in a park or a field. ..............................
3. This is what you put in a bin. You shouldn't leave it on the ground or throw it in lakes. ..............................
4. Many people like this sport. They do it in winter. They sit or lie down to do it. ..............................
5. You should recycle these when you have finished drinking from them. ..............................
6. They fly with four wings. They can be purple, red or other colours. They are insects. ..............................
7. They are disappearing very quickly but there is still time to help them. They can be birds, animals or insects. ..............................
8. We often play outside in this season because it's warm and sunny. It's before autumn. ..............................
9. Some animals and insects have got lines on them. Tigers and zebras are like this. ..............................
10. We usually do these sports outside. They can be running, jumping or throwing. ..............................

**2** **Kim is asking Mr Green some questions about the environment. What does Mr Green say? Read the conversation and choose the best answer. Write a letter (A–H) for each answer. You do not need to use all the letters.**

*Example*

**Kim:** Excuse me, Mr Green. Can I ask you some questions about the environment? It's for my ezine project.

**Mr Green:** ....C....

*Questions*

1

**Kim:** When did you become interested in the environment?

**Mr Green:** ............

2

**Kim:** Have you ever written a book about the environment?

**Mr Green:** ............

3

**Kim:** What can we do to save trees?

**Mr Green:** ............

4

**Kim:** How many endangered species are there today?

**Mr Green:** ............

5

**Kim:** Thank you very much, Mr Green.

**Mr Green:** ............

**A** Yes. I've written two about recycling.

**B** Yes it is. I've won a prize.

**C** Of course. How can I help you? (***Example***)

**D** You're welcome, Kim. Good luck!

**E** You shouldn't throw paper away. Recycle it!

**F** You should build bird houses and plant flowers.

**G** I've wanted to learn about it since I was a young boy.

**H** A lot. And every year there are more.

## 3 Read the story. Choose a word from the box. Write the correct word next to numbers 1–5. There is one example.

| *example* | | | | | |
|---|---|---|---|---|---|
| ~~left~~ | hurting | used | cream | walk | forgot |
| wanted | wear | yellow | sing | | |

Yesterday Peter, Mary and John went walking in the hills. Before they ........left........ the house, their mother said, 'Peter, you should put a hat on.' 'Yes, Mum,' he replied. 'John, you should **(1)** ........................ trainers.'

'Yes, Mum,' he replied. 'Mary, don't forget to put on your sun **(2)** ........................ if it gets hot.' 'Yes, Mum,' Mary replied. But Peter hates hats, so he didn't take one. John doesn't like trainers, so he wore plastic shoes and Mary **(3)** ........................ to take the cream.

At midday they reached the top of a hill. The sun was very hot and Mary's arms were red. 'I feel sick,' said Peter. 'I feel sick too,' said Mary. John's foot was **(4)** ........................ . But there was nowhere to hide from the sun.

When they got home, they went to bed. The next day Peter was ill and couldn't play in his football game, Mary's arms were red and burnt and John couldn't **(5)** ........................ on his bad foot.

'You should listen to me,' said Mum.

'Yes, Mum,' they replied.

**(6) Now choose the best name for the story. Tick (✓) one box.**

A sunny day ☐ Listen to your mother ☐ Feeling sick ☐

## 4 Read the text. Choose the right words and write them on the lines.

### Endangered animals

*Example* Every day more and ...more... animals are becoming extinct.

1 In some countries people are .................... endangered animals.

2 .................... example, national parks look after tigers in Russia.

3 They understand that there are people .................... want their fur.

4 Frogs are in danger all over .................... world. To make us think

5 .................... frogs more, people named 2008 'Year of the Frog'.

6 Every year millions of Purple Spotted Butterflies ....................

7 because they fly .................... roads and cars hit them.

8 In 2007 .................... Taiwan, they started to close the busy roads and now the butterflies are protected. There are still more

9 .................... 1,000 endangered insects and animals but people

10 .................... helping to save them!

| | | | |
|---|---|---|---|
| *Example* | more | many | most |
| 1 | protects | protected | protecting |
| 2 | For | By | At |
| 3 | we | who | what |
| 4 | a | one | the |
| 5 | with | about | over |
| 6 | died | dies | die |
| 7 | near | out | straight |
| 8 | from | to | in |
| 9 | of | than | as |
| 10 | aren't | is | are |

**5** **Look at the picture and read the story. Write some words to complete the sentences about the story. You can use 1, 2, 3 or 4 words.**

## Alex and the bull

Last summer Mr and Mrs Short took their two sons, Jack and Alex, to the countryside for a picnic. It was a lovely sunny day.

The family found a large field and sat down on the grass. They put their picnic on a big red blanket on the grass. They were hungry, so they ate their sandwiches quickly. Then they had some biscuits and drank some orange juice.

When Dad was putting their rubbish into the bin, he heard a loud noise. 'Be careful!' he shouted. 'It's a bull.' The bull was very angry and it was coming after them.

The family didn't know what to do. Jack, the older boy, climbed up a tree. Dad hid behind the rubbish bin. Mum ran across the field. But where was little Alex? They couldn't see him. But Alex was hiding under the red blanket. And now the angry bull was near him.

Suddenly Alex moved a little bit. The bull couldn't see Alex's head, his arms or legs. He only saw that the red blanket was moving. The bull was really scared and ran away. Everyone was safe.

'Well done, Alex!' said Dad. 'You saved us. Did you know that bulls don't like the colour red?' Alex didn't know. But he knows now!

### *Examples*

The Short family had ......a picnic...... in the countryside.

The weather was ......sunny...... .

### *Questions*

1 They put the red blanket on ............................ .

2 The family ate quickly because they were ............................ .

3 Dad heard ............................ when he was putting rubbish in the bin.

4 Jack climbed up ............................ .

5 Mum ran to the other side of the ............................ .

6 They couldn't ............................ Alex.

7 The bull ran away because bulls don't like ............................ .

 

## 6 Read the letter and write the missing words. Write one word on each line.

Dear James,

***Example*** I'm ...having... a wonderful holiday.

1 Yesterday I .................... snowboarding and sledging with my

2 sister. And guess what! I've learnt to ski! Have you ....................

been skiing? Yesterday I went downhill. I'm not very good

3 .................... skiing but I love it.

4 My sister is really good! .................... Sunday she was in a race

and she won a medal!

In the evening we went to a restaurant to celebrate.

5 Do you .................... skiing?

Love,

Ben

**7** **Look at the three pictures. Write about this story. Write 20 or more words.**

---

 

# Test Units 7-8

**Speaking**

**1**

Teacher's card

**Find the Differences**

Pupil's card

**Find the Differences**

2

Teacher's card

**Tom**

| | |
|---|---|
| What sport / play | ? |
| How often / practise | ? |
| What / won | ? |
| How old / when started playing | ? |
| Been skiing | ? |

**Sarah**

| | |
|---|---|
| What sport / play | badminton |
| How often / practise | 2 nights a week |
| What / won | a silver medal |
| How old / when started playing | 7 |
| Been skiing | yes |

**Find Information. Ask and answer.**

Pupil's card

**Tom**

| | |
|---|---|
| What sport / play | tennis |
| How often / practise | 3 days a week |
| What / won | a gold medal |
| How old / when started playing | 8 |
| Been skiing | no |

**Sarah**

| | |
|---|---|
| What sport / play | ? |
| How often / practise | ? |
| What / won | ? |
| How old / when started playing | ? |
| Been skiing | ? |

**Find Information. Ask and answer.**

 

# 3 Robert goes cycling

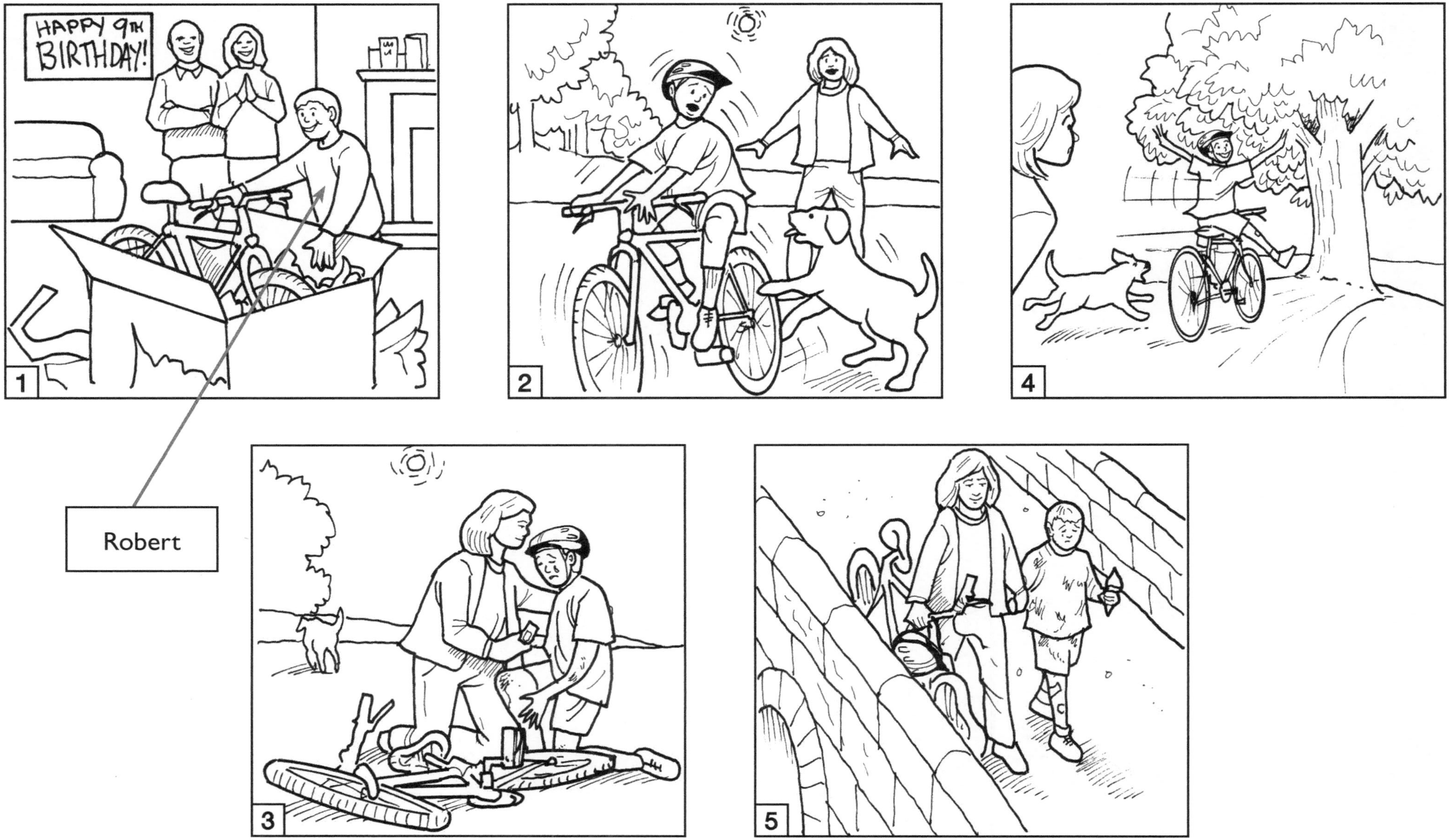


## Tell the Story

# Test key and audioscripts

Marks are not shown on the tests themselves, giving you the flexibility to mark in a way that suits your teaching situation. However, a scheme is given below which you may wish to use. Note that all four skills carry equal weight in the *Cambridge English: Young Learners* Tests. There are four complete tests in this section.

## Marking Key

( ) = Acceptable extra words are placed in brackets
/ = A single slash is placed between acceptable alternative words within an answer
// = A double slash is placed between acceptable alternative complete answers

**Listening Key:** F = adult female, M = adult male, FCH = female child, MCH = male child.

## Test Units Welcome–2 pp 76–90

### Listening Part 1 (5 marks): page 76

**Key:** Lines should be drawn as follows:

1 Betty and girl writing at the desk, wearing a jacket
2 Harry and boy wearing pilot's uniform, carrying a plane
3 Sarah and shorter nurse, wearing glasses
4 Emma and girl dressed as fire fighter, carrying hat, no shoes
5 Richard and boy on floor looking at plants

TRACK 16

*Part One. Look at the picture. Listen and look. There is one example.*

F: Hello Mr Green.
M: Hello, Mrs Smith. Why are all the children in uniform?
F: They're wearing clothes for the jobs they're going to do.
M: I see. Where's my son, David?
F: He's there look. He's sitting on the floor. He's a mechanic.
M: Oh yes. What's he doing?
F: He's working on a toy car.

*Can you see the line? This is an example. Now you listen and draw lines.*

M: Who are the other children here?
F: Can you see the girl with blonde hair?
M: Is she writing in a notebook?
F: That's right. And she's wearing a jacket. That's Betty.
M: Does she want to be a journalist?
F: Yes. She's very good at English.
F: And can you see that boy in a hat? His name's Harry.
M: Is he carrying a plane under his arm?
F: Yes. His dad's a pilot and he wants to be one too.
M: And who's the girl who's talking to my son?
F: The tall girl with blonde hair?
M: No. I mean the short girl. She's dressed as a nurse too, but she's wearing glasses.
F: Oh, yes. I see her. That's Sarah. She and your son do maths together.
M: Is a girl called Emma here today?
F: Yes, she's a fire fighter. Can you see her hat?
M: Is she wearing it?
F: No, it's really heavy. She's carrying it in her hand.
M: Why hasn't she got any shoes on?
F: She stood in some water and they're wet.
M: I think I know that boy with the bowl. He lives in our street.
F: The other boy on the floor?
M: Yes. Is his name Richard?
F: Yes. He's a very good football player.
M: But he's not dressed as one today.
F: That's right. He loves working with plants and animals. He wants to be a scientist.

### Listening Part 2 (5 marks): page 77

**Key:** 1 13, 2 School, 3 White, 4 Saturday, 5 3.15//quarter past three.

TRACK 17

*Part Two. Listen and look. There is one example.*

F: Hello. Thank you for calling. Can I have your name, please?
MCH: Yes. It's Peter Clark.
F: Clark. Is that C-L-A-R-K?
MCH: Yes. I'd like to be an actor in your new TV series.

*Can you see the answer? Now you listen and write.*

F: And how old are you Peter?
MCH: I'm 13. It was my birthday last week.
F: Did you have a nice birthday?
MCH: Yes, thank you.
F: Now what kind of things do you watch on television, Peter?
MCH: Well, I like documentaries. There's a really good one called *Animal World* and I often watch cartoons too. But my favourite is your TV series *School is Cool*.
F: OK, I've got that. And who's your favourite movie actor?
MCH: Well, there are lots of great movie and TV actors. But I think the best actor in the world is Will Black. I'm sorry, I mean Will *White*! His movies are great.
F: Well, Peter. We'd like you to do some acting for us. When can you come to Channel 3?
MCH: Is it possible to come on Sunday?
F: I'm sorry. More than 20 children are going to come on that day.
MCH: Oh, I see. Is Saturday OK then?
F: Yes, that's fine.
MCH: What time shall I come? My mum says any time is OK.
F: Can I put your name down for quarter past three?
MCH: Yes, thank you.
F: OK, Peter. We'll see you at the weekend.
MCH: Thank you very much. Goodbye.

### Listening Part 3 (5 marks): page 78

**Key:** 1 B Mary and history, 2 G Katy and English, 3 D Emma and music, 4 C Bill and science, 5 F Tom and art.

TRACK 18

*Part Three. Listen and look. There is one example. What is each pupil's favourite school subject?*

F: Daisy. Tell me about your classmates. What are their favourite school subjects?
FCH: Let me see. Ben likes sport best. He plays badminton every Wednesday and he plays football every day. He says he's going to be a footballer one day.

*Can you see the letter E next to Ben? Now you listen and write a letter in each box.*

F: Does anyone in your class like history?
FCH: Only one person.
F: Who's that?
FCH: Mary! She says that the teacher's really nice and she likes learning about the past. But the other people in my class think it's better to learn about living now.

**F:** What about your friend, Katy? What does she like?
**FCH:** Well, she wants to go to different countries.
**F:** Oh. So does she like geography?
**FCH:** She thinks it's OK. But she loves speaking to people from other countries, so she likes languages best. She's got a big English dictionary. That's her favourite language.
**F:** What about Emma? She's got a new computer, hasn't she? Does she like computer science?
**FCH:** She thinks the classes are very difficult and there's a lot of homework. She prefers music. She loves playing the guitar.
**F:** What other subjects do you study?
**FCH:** Well, lots of people like science and it's Bill's favourite subject. He loves learning about animals. But he doesn't understand when the teacher talks about plants.
**F:** And what about art? Does anyone like those classes?
**FCH:** Oh yes! Lots of people like them. Tom really likes painting and drawing. He's good at taking photos too.
**F:** Well, that's good. Your school sounds very nice.

## Listening Part 4 (5 marks): page 79

**Key:** 1 B, 2 C, 3 B, 4 A, 5 A.

TRACK 19

*Part Four. Listen and look. There is one example.*
*Where's Ben's mum going to work?*

**FCH:** Hi Ben. How are you?
**MCH:** I'm really excited. My mum's going to start a new job!
**FCH:** Where's she going to work?
**MCH:** Well, she wanted to work in a TV studio but now she's got a job in the School of Archaeology at the university.
**FCH:** My dad works there, in the School of Art.

*Can you see the tick? Now you listen and tick the box.*

1 *What job is Ben's mum going to do?*
**FCH:** Is your mum going to be a scientist and study bones?
**MCH:** No, she's going to draw pictures of them.
**FCH:** Really? That's cool. But don't they do that on computers?
**MCH:** Sometimes. But Mum does it with a pencil.

2 *Who's Ben's mum going to work for?*
**MCH:** Mum's going to work for a famous archaeologist!
**FCH:** Really? Is she going to work for Diggory Bones?
**MCH:** No, she's going to work for his brother, Archie Bones.
**FCH:** He isn't famous.
**MCH:** Yes, he is. He's more famous than Diggory Bones! And he's more famous than Doug Bones too.

3 *When's Ben's mum going to start her new job?*
**FCH:** When is your mum going to start her new job?
**MCH:** Well, she wanted to start on 1 July, but she can't.
**FCH:** Why not?
**MCH:** Because she has to work in her old job then.
**FCH:** Oh.
**MCH:** Yeah, but it's really exciting because she can start on 15 July and then on 21 July the School of Archaeology is going to be in a TV programme!

4 *What kind of TV programme is the School of Archaeology going to be in?*
**FCH:** Wow! Is the programme a documentary?
**MCH:** No. I asked her that. And it's not a quiz.
**FCH:** Oh. What is it then?
**MCH:** It's part of a sports programme. They want to show people that running and jumping can give you strong bones.

5 *What's Ben's mum's job now?*
**FCH:** Your mum's a dentist now, isn't she?
**MCH:** No, that's my dad. My mum's a history teacher.
**FCH:** Oh right. Well, she's going to be on TV, so perhaps she's going to be a famous actress now!

## Listening Part 5 (5 marks): page 80

**Key:** 1 green chair by the board, 2 blue English dictionary on the big desk, 3 yellow paper on the left of the wall, 4 PROJECT written on poster next to bookcase, 5 FRIDAY on board.

TRACK 20

*Part Five. Listen and look at the picture. There is one example.*

**M:** Can you help me with this picture of a classroom?
**FCH:** All right. What shall I do?
**M:** Can you see the door?
**FCH:** Yes, I can.
**M:** OK. Well, colour it black.
**FCH:** Right. I'm doing that now.

*Can you see the black door? This is an example.*
*Now you listen and colour and write.*

1
**M:** How many chairs can you see?
**FCH:** I can see six.
**M:** That's right. Can you see the one next to the board?
**FCH:** Yes. I think it's for the teacher. Shall I colour it?
**M:** What colour do you think she'd like?
**FCH:** Green, I think.
**M:** Good idea. Do it that colour.

2
**M:** Now look at the teacher's table. What can you see there?
**FCH:** There's a pen, an eraser and a notebook.
**M:** And can you see the dictionaries?
**FCH:** Yes, I can. There are two.
**M:** That's right. Can you colour the English dictionary?
**FCH:** What colour?
**M:** Colour it blue.
**FCH:** OK.

3
**M:** What can you see between the door and the bookcase?
**FCH:** There are two pieces of paper on the wall.
**M:** Good. Now colour one of them.
**FCH:** Which one?
**M:** The one which is on the left.
**FCH:** OK. I'm going to do it yellow.

4
**M:** Can you write something now?
**FCH:** Yes, OK!
**M:** Can you write on the poster next to the bookcase?
**FCH:** Yes. What shall I write?
**M:** Write the word PROJECT on it. You're going to do one in class soon!
**FCH:** Yes, we are. OK, I've written that now.
**M:** Well done.

5
**M:** What else do we need in the picture?
**FCH:** In my classroom, the teacher usually writes the day of the week on the board.
**M:** OK. Let's write that. What day is it today?
**FCH:** It's Friday.
**M:** Write that on the board.
**FCH:** Great. Soon it will be the weekend!

## Reading & Writing Part 1 (10 marks): page 81

**Key:** 1 a dictionary, 2 cartoons, 3 a fire fighter, 4 science, 5 pilots, 6 history, 7 geography, 8 dentists, 9 the news, 10 an ezine.

### Reading & Writing Part 2 (5 marks): page 82

**Key:** 1 G, 2 B, 3 F, 4 A, 5 D.

### Reading & Writing Part 3 (6 marks): page 83

**Key:** 1 newspaper, 2 forty//40, 3 quickly, 4 phone, 5 important, 6 A fire in the park.

### Reading & Writing Part 4 (10 marks): page 84

**Key:** 1 Do, 2 When, 3 there, 4 using, 5 every, 6 on, 7 should, 8 called, 9 wins, 10 Why

### Reading & Writing Part 5 (7 marks): page 85

**Key:** 1 Monday and Friday, 2 a (great) singer, 3 September, 4 six//6, 5 school, 6 well, 7 second prize.

### Reading & Writing Part 6 (5 marks): page 86

**Key:** 1 see//watch//catch, 2 asked, 3 had, 4 an, 5 of.

### Reading & Writing Part 7 (5 marks): page 87

**Key:** Pupils' own answers

### Speaking: pages 88–90

- Part 1. See general notes (page 6) in the Introduction for how to set up this part of the Speaking test. Give an example. Aim to elicit six differences from the pupil.
- Part 2. See general notes. Start by introducing Nick. *This is Nick. I don't know anything about him but you do. So I'm going to ask you some questions. How old is Nick?* Ask pupils to answer the questions about Nick, then say *Now you ask me questions about Jenny* and point to the prompts on the Pupil's card.
- Part 3. See general notes. Start the story *It's Tuesday. There's going to be a science test on Friday. Michael wants to get 20 out of 20.*
- Part 4. Follow on the theme of what the pupil does in the evening by asking questions such as: *What do you do in the evenings? What do you eat? Do you watch TV? Do you play sport? What time do you go to bed?*

## Test Units 3–4 pp 91–105

### Listening Part 1 (5 marks): page 91

**Key:** Lines should be drawn as follows:
1 Robert and boy on bridge, looking at cap in river
2 Michael and boy with long hair carrying a guitar
3 Helen and girl with short hair, in jacket and jeans, going into the theatre
4 Jack and boy on bench with notebook in hand
5 Bill and boy outside café, sitting with his dad, paying the waiter

**TRACK 21**

*Part One. Look at the picture. Listen and look. There is one example.*

**FCH:** Thanks for bringing me out tonight, Dad. It's really exciting. Lots of my friends are going to the theatre.
**M:** That's good.
**FCH:** Oh look! There's my friend Anna!
**M:** The girl in the black shirt?
**FCH:** Yes. She's walking across the street to the theatre.

*Can you see the line? This is an example. Now you listen and draw lines.*

**M:** What about Robert? Is he here yet?
**FCH:** I don't think so. He's always late!
**M:** Wait! That's him, over there!
**FCH:** Where?
**M:** He's on the bridge. Can you see him? He's looking at something in the river.
**FCH:** Oh, yes. Look. His hat's fallen into the water.
**M:** Oh dear.
**M:** And who's that boy?
**FCH:** Do you mean the boy who's carrying a guitar?
**M:** Yes.
**FCH:** That's Michael. He's going to play in the theatre. He's very good at music.
**M:** But look at his hair! It's very long!
**FCH:** Lots of boys have long hair these days, Dad.
**FCH:** Look! There's Helen. She's going into the theatre.
**M:** Do you mean the girl who's wearing a dress?
**FCH:** No, she's wearing jeans and a jacket.
**M:** She's got short hair. Do all your girl friends have short hair and the boys have long hair?
**FCH:** No, Dad!
**M:** Can you see any other friends?
**FCH:** Yes. There's one boy from my class sitting in the street.
**M:** Oh, yes. That's Jack, isn't it?
**FCH:** That's right.
**M:** Why has he got a notebook in his hand?
**FCH:** He's probably going to draw pictures!
**M:** In the street?
**FCH:** Yes. He *loves* art! He draws everything.
**M:** Where's your friend Bill? Is he coming to the theatre?
**FCH:** He's in that café.
**M:** Is he sitting with his mum?
**FCH:** No. He's with his dad. And he's giving money to the waiter.

### Listening Part 2 (5 marks): page 92

**Key:** 1 11//eleven, 2 Clock, 3 (her) aunt, 4 Saturday, 5 Walkers.

**TRACK 22**

*Part Two. Listen and look. There is one example.*

**F:** Excuse me. Can I ask you about your visit to London?
**FCH:** Yes, of course. What do you want to know?
**F:** What's your name, please?
**FCH:** It's Sarah Perez.
**F:** Perez. Is that P-E-R-E-Z?
**FCH:** Yes, that's right.

*Can you see the answer? Now you listen and write.*

**F:** Why are you in London, Sarah?
**FCH:** It's my birthday! We're going to go to London Zoo this morning.
**F:** Happy birthday! How old are you?
**FCH:** I'm 11 today.
**F:** That's great!
**F:** Where are you staying, Sarah? In a hotel?
**FCH:** Yes, we are.
**F:** And what's the name of the hotel?
**FCH:** It's called The Clock Hotel.
**F:** Oh, I know that. It's one of the oldest hotels in London.
**F:** And who are you in London with?
**FCH:** I'm here with my aunt.
**F:** Oh, so that woman's not your mum.
**FCH:** No, she couldn't come to London.
**F:** Why's that?
**FCH:** She's working. She can't have a holiday this month.
**F:** Now, how many days are you staying in London, Sarah?
**FCH:** We're here for six days.
**F:** When did you arrive?
**FCH:** Yesterday.
**F:** That's Monday. So you're going home on Saturday?
**FCH:** Yes. That's right.

**F:** And where are you going this afternoon?
**FCH:** To a toy shop. I'm going to buy a birthday present.
**F:** That's nice. What's the name of the shop?
**FCH:** Walkers.
**F:** I don't know that shop. Please can you spell it for me?
**FCH:** Yes. It's W-A-L-K-E-R-S. Walkers.
**F:** Thanks. Well, I hope you enjoy your time here in London.
**FCH:** Thank you.

## Listening Part 3 (5 marks): page 93

**Key:** 1 B William and leaves on fire, 2 E David and boy looking for watch in coat pocket, 3 G Mary and broken tooth, 4 H Jane and hurt leg, 5 D Alex and cut finger.

TRACK 23

*Part Three. Listen and look. There is one example. What happened to the pupils in Robert's class?*

**M:** Hello Robert. Did you have a good day at school today?
**MCH:** Yes, it was fun. We learned about disasters in history.
**M:** The children in your class have a lot of disasters, don't they?
**MCH:** Yes. Do you remember what happened to Vicky last year?
**M:** Yes. That was a terrible accident. She was sailing with her dad when some lightning hit the boat. They jumped in the water and a helicopter came to get them.

*Can you see the letter F next to Vicky? Now you listen and write a letter in each box.*

**M:** And another friend had an accident last November, didn't he?
**MCH:** Oh yes. William and his friends were jumping in some leaves in the garden. His dad was burning things and the leaves caught fire. The boys had to go to the hospital. But they were OK.
**M:** That was lucky.
**MCH:** But one of the boys wasn't lucky.
**M:** Why?
**MCH:** Well, when they were jumping in the leaves, David put his watch in his coat pocket. He thought about it the next day but it wasn't there. So he lost it.
**M:** Oh dear.
**MCH:** And then there was Mary.
**M:** What happened to her?
**MCH:** She was going downstairs. Her little brother's toy car was there. She put her foot on it and she fell.
**M:** Did she break her arm?
**MCH:** No, she broke her tooth. She couldn't smile!
**MCH:** And her sister Jane fell down the next day too.
**M:** Really?
**MCH:** Yes. She was climbing up a tree and it was really wet. She fell onto the ground and she hurt her leg. She couldn't play football or volleyball for four weeks.
**M:** And did your friend Alex have an accident too?
**MCH:** Oh yes. He wanted to make a sandwich for lunch. He was cutting the bread with a big knife and he cut his finger.
**M:** Right. Well, I'm going to make some sandwiches for us now. But don't worry. I'll be careful!
**MCH:** That's good, Dad!

## Listening Part 4 (5 marks): page 94

**Key:** 1 C, 2 B, 3 B, 4 A, 5 C.

TRACK 24

*Part Four. Listen and look. There is one example.*
*Where in town was the fire?*

**M:** Did you hear about the fire in town yesterday?
**F:** Was it in the clothes shop like last year?
**M:** No, it was in a café. But nobody was hurt. The fire fighters came from the fire station very quickly.
**F:** That's good.

*Can you see the tick? Now you listen and tick the box.*

1 *Where was the café?*
**F:** Which café was it?
**M:** You know if you go from the train station straight up the High Street?
**F:** Yes?
**M:** Well, it's in the first street on the left.
**F:** Oh yes. I know. That's Mr Green's café. But it's not my favourite. I like the one that's in the first street on the right. I go there with my friend on Friday mornings.

2 *Where did the fire start?*
**F:** And where did the fire start? Was it in the kitchen?
**M:** No, it was because of the storm yesterday evening. The lightning hit the building.
**F:** That happened to me last year and my computer caught fire.
**M:** Well this fire started because the lightning hit the clock on the wall outside.
**F:** Wow! That's a surprise.

3 *What was Mr Green doing when the fire started?*
**F:** Was Mr Green in the café when the fire started?
**M:** Yes, he was. He was talking.
**F:** On the phone? That's dangerous when there's a storm.
**M:** He was talking to one of his customers, Mrs Smith. She goes shopping and then goes to the café for a cup of tea.

4 *What did the customers do when the fire started?*
**F:** Did the customers run out into the street?
**M:** You shouldn't run when there's a fire. No, they were very good. They all walked out of the café and went home.
**F:** Didn't anyone stand in the street and watch?
**M:** It was raining a lot so I don't think they wanted to do that.

5 *Where did the man hear about the fire?*
**F:** How do you know about the fire? There wasn't anything on the TV last night.
**M:** I know. My friend told me about it.
**F:** Well, perhaps it's going to be on the radio news today.

## Listening Part 5 (5 marks): page 95

**Key:** 1 a green castle door next to the police officer, 2 a red small coffee cup, 3 PIZZA written on the board outside the café, 4 blue T-shirt on boy listening to music, 5 AUGUST written on the sign above 'Park'

TRACK 25

*Part five. Listen and look at the picture. There is one example.*

**M:** Can you help me with this picture? Can you see the castle?
**FCH:** Yes. It looks very strong.
**M:** Yes, it does. Can you colour it grey?
**FCH:** OK. That's a good colour for a castle.

*Can you see the grey castle? This is an example.*
*Now you listen and colour and write.*

1
**M:** Now can you colour the castle door?
**FCH:** Which one do you mean?
**M:** The one where the police officer is standing.
**FCH:** Oh, OK.
**M:** Why don't you colour it green?
**FCH:** Right. I'm doing that now.

2
**M:** Now look at the café. Can you see the two women sitting outside? They're both drinking coffee.
**FCH:** Yes, I can see them.
**M:** Why don't you colour one of their coffee cups?
**FCH:** OK. Shall I colour the one next to the piece of cake?
**M:** No. Colour the other one.
**FCH:** Right. I think I'll colour it red.
**M:** That's a good idea.

**3**

**M:** I think you can have something to eat here too. Look, the cook's going to write something on the board outside.

**FCH:** Oh yes. What do you think he's going to write?

**M:** I think it's PIZZA. Do you want to write it for him?

**FCH:** OK.

**4**

**M:** Can you see those boys? You could colour one of their T-shirts.

**FCH:** OK. I'm going to colour the T-shirt of the boy listening to music.

**M:** What colour are you going to do it?

**FCH:** I'm going to do it blue.

**5**

**FCH:** It looks nice where the boys are, doesn't it?

**M:** Yes, it does. Why don't you write the name? It's called August Park.

**FCH:** Oh, like the month?

**M:** Exactly.

**FCH:** OK. I'm writing that now.

**M:** Excellent. What a great picture!

## Reading & Writing Part 1 (10 marks): page 96

**Key:** 1 a bridge, 2 a castle, 3 October, 4 fire stations, 5 December, 6 museums, 7 July, 8 an airport, 9 a cinema, 10 February.

## Reading & Writing Part 2 (5 marks): page 97

**Key:** 1 H, 2 D, 3 A, 4 F, 5 G.

## Reading & Writing Part 3 (6 marks): page 98

**Key:** 1 paintings, 2 across, 3 most, 4 minutes, 5 fall, 6 An exciting story.

## Reading & Writing Part 4 (10 marks): page 99

**Key:** 1 this, 2 sailing, 3 on, 4 there, 5 or, 6 came, 7 into, 8 waited, 9 her, 10 worst.

## Reading & Writing Part 5 (7 marks): page 100

**Key:** 1 three/3 friends, 2 half an hour//30 minutes, 3 11.00// eleven/11 o'clock, 4 fell in(to) 5 swim (very well), 6 terrible 7 June.

## Reading & Writing Part 6 (5 marks): page 101

**Key:** 1 on, 2 had, 3 second//2nd, 4 to, 5 tell.

## Reading & Writing Part 7 (5 marks): page 102

**Key:** Pupils' own answers

## Speaking: pages 103–105

- Part 1. See general notes (page 6) in the Introduction for how to set up this part of the Speaking test. Give an example. Aim to elicit six differences from the pupil.
- Part 2. See general notes. Introduce Mary. Say *This is Mary. She went out this morning. I don't know anything about her but you do. I'm going to ask you some questions. Where did Mary go this morning?* Ask the pupil to answer all the questions about Mary then say, *Now you ask me questions about Richard.* Point to the prompts on the Pupil's card.
- Part 3. See general notes. Start the story *Yesterday, Fred was out in the park with his dog.*
- Part 4. Follow on the theme of going out in the town by asking *Where do you like to go in the town? Do you go to the park? What do you do there? Do you go shopping? What do you buy? Do you like museums?*

# Test Units 5-6 pp 106-120

## Listening Part 1 (5 marks): page 106

**Key:** Lines should be drawn as follows:

1 Fred and man sitting on chair, reading old newspapers
2 Lucy and girl next to food bin, drinking from a bottle
3 Sarah and woman in dress with box of plastic
4 Alex and man with wooden box, looking worried
5 Jim and boy with rucksack on back, climbing onto metal bin

**TRACK 26**

*Part One. Look at the picture. Listen and look. There is one example.*

**F:** Thanks for coming to help, Tom.

**MCH:** There are a lot of people here today, aren't there?

**F:** Yes, and I know them all. … Right, over there is the paper bin. We put newspapers, card and old paper in there.

**MCH:** Who's the woman who's standing by that bin?

**F:** That's Mary. She comes here every week.

**MCH:** But she's going to put metal in it! That's not right!

**F:** No. She's going to need some help.

*Can you see the line? This is an example. Now you listen and draw lines.*

**MCH:** Who's that man? He's sitting on the chair.

**F:** Oh, that's Fred. He comes every week too.

**MCH:** What is he doing?

**F:** He's just reading the old newspapers. He doesn't put anything in the bins!

**F:** Now … the bin for old food is on the right.

**MCH:** Who's the girl next to it?

**F:** The one eating an apple?

**MCH:** No, she's drinking something – from a glass bottle.

**F:** Oh. That's Lucy.

**MCH:** I hope she's not going to put her bottle in that bin!

**F:** People are putting a lot of things into the plastic bin today. Look at Sarah.

**MCH:** But she's only got one plastic bag.

**F:** No, not her, the other woman. She's wearing a dress. Look at the box by her feet.

**MCH:** Wow! She's got lots of plastic!

**F:** Yes. Her family eats a lot of food!

**MCH:** Does that man know what to do?

**F:** Which one?

**MCH:** He's holding a wooden box.

**F:** Oh, that's Alex.

**MCH:** Is he OK? I think he's looking for something.

**F:** Yes. He recycles everything! And he puts it all in the right place, but I think he's lost his son.

**MCH:** What's his son's name?

**F:** It's Jim.

**MCH:** The boy with the rucksack on his back?

**F:** Yes. Oh dear! He's climbing on the metal recycling bin! Quick! Stop him!

**MCH:** OK. I'm going now. Hey!

## Listening Part 2 (5 marks): page 107

**Key:** 1 school, 2 Children, 3 spiders, 4 120, 5 845 3790.

**TRACK 27**

*Part Two. Listen and look. There is one example.*

**M:** Hello. Are you Katy Barker?

**FCH:** Yes, I am.

**M:** I'm from the town newspaper. We'd like to write about your special birthday party next month. Can you spell your surname, Barker, for me please?

**FCH:** Yes, it's B-A-R-K-E-R.
**M:** Thank you.

*Can you see the answer? Now you listen and write.*

**M:** Tell me about your party.
**FCH:** It's going to be different from other parties.
**M:** Why?
**FCH:** Because we're going to sell food not eat it.
**M:** And where are you going to do that? At home?
**FCH:** At school. My teacher says it's OK.
**M:** And how did you have the idea?
**FCH:** Well, it started in my geography class.
**M:** Oh, yes?
**FCH:** Yes. We learnt that lots of people in the world are hungry. So we're going to sell food to get some money.
**M:** Who will you give the money to?
**FCH:** It's called 'Help the Children'. They give two meals a day to children who haven't got very much food.
**M:** It's a great idea. What are you going to cook?
**FCH:** I'm going to make chocolate spiders. But other people are going to make cakes and biscuits.
**M:** I'd like to buy some!
**M:** And how many people are going to be at the party?
**FCH:** There are about 30 children in my class but people from other classes can come too.
**M:** So it's for all the school?
**FCH:** Yes. I think about 120 people are going to be there.
**M:** Really? It's going to be great!
**M:** What's your phone number? We can talk again after the party.
**FCH:** It's 8453790.
**M:** Thank you and good luck, Katy!

## Listening Part 3 (5 marks): page 108

**Key:** 1 G Katy and hand recording family singing, 2 B David and baby made of shapes, 3 H Richard and sweets, 4 A Sally and picture of smelly cheese, 5 F John and bicycle.

TRACK 28

*Part Three. Listen and look. There is one example. What did the children in the class make?*

**F:** What are all these things in your classroom?
**FCH:** Oh, we're studying the senses. We had to make something about a sense.
**F:** So, what did you make, Anna?
**FCH:** I chose the sense of touch, so this is my project.
**F:** It looks like an animal.
**FCH:** Yes, it's a tiger. I made it with fur. It feels nice.

*Can you see the letter D next to Anna? Now you listen and write a letter in each box.*

**F:** Tell me about the other people in your class. Did anyone choose the sense of hearing?
**FCH:** Yes. This is Katy's project. She made a CD with sounds of people in her family. You can hear her mum, her dad and her sisters. They're talking and singing. And you can hear her little baby sister too. She sounds really angry!
**F:** Which is David's project?
**FCH:** His project's a picture about the sense of sight. He's using three shapes: circles, triangles and squares.
**F:** Is his picture a house?
**FCH:** No, it's a baby with a hat on.
**F:** I think the hat looks like a roof, don't you?
**FCH:** Yes, it does.
**F:** What about taste? Who chose that?
**FCH:** Oh, that's Richard. Can you see? His project's a box with food in it. He made it all. There are some sweets, some chocolate and some cake. The sweets taste really nice!
**F:** Did Sally choose taste too?
**FCH:** Why?
**F:** Well, there's a picture of some cheese with her name on it.
**FCH:** Oh no! Her project's about smell. That cheese was really strong. It was horrible. It smelled like old socks! We had to open the classroom windows all morning.
**F:** And what's John's project?
**FCH:** He's really clever. He's making a bicycle. It's made of recycled metal and it can move! But it sounds strange when you move it. It sounds like an old car!

## Listening Part 4 (5 marks): page 109

**Key:** 1 C, 2 A, 3 B, 4 A, 5 C.

TRACK 29

*Part Four. Listen and look. There is one example. Where was Jason's birthday party?*

**F:** How was your birthday, Jason?
**MCH:** Fine thanks, Grandma.
**F:** Did you spend the day at home?
**MCH:** No, we didn't.
**F:** Did you go to the cinema?
**MCH:** No. We had a party at a restaurant.
**F:** That's nice.

*Can you see the tick? Now you listen and tick the box.*

1 *Why didn't Grandma go to the birthday party?*

**F:** I'm sorry I couldn't come to your party, Jason.
**MCH:** It's OK, Grandma. You were ill.
**F:** No. I wasn't ill. Your grandfather was ill.
**MCH:** Really? Is he all right now?
**F:** He's fine. He's working in the garden today.

2 *What did Jason eat?*

**F:** What did you eat at the party?
**MCH:** Well, there were chips, salad and pasta.
**F:** That's nice. What did you have?
**MCH:** I didn't have any pasta.
**F:** Why?
**MCH:** I wasn't very hungry. So I just ate some chips.
**F:** Did they taste nice?
**MCH:** They tasted OK. But they smelt horrible.

3 *What did the birthday cake look like?*

**F:** Did you have a birthday cake?
**MCH:** Well yes, but there was a problem. Mum bought one from a shop. It was very funny.
**F:** Why?
**MCH:** It had a doll who was dancing on the top!
**F:** Couldn't your mum find a cake that looked like a train or a football?
**MCH:** No. The shop didn't have any others. But it tasted nice. And everyone sang 'Happy Birthday'.

4 *What was Jason's favourite present?*

**F:** What presents did you get?
**MCH:** My parents bought me a really nice book about science. And my friends bought me a toy spider.
**F:** That's nice. What was your favourite present?
**MCH:** Your present, Grandma!
**F:** Really? You like the watch?
**MCH:** I love it, thank you. Look. I'm wearing it now.

5 *When is Jason going to visit his grandparents?*

**F:** When can you come to see us, Jason? On Thursday?
**MCH:** Saturday's better. You see, I've got an exam at school on Friday, so it's not a good idea to come before that.
**F:** Fine. Make sure you're hungry! I'm going to cook you a big meal and make you a cake too.
**MCH:** Thank you!

## Listening Part 5 (5 marks): page 110

**Key:** 1 COOK written on the cat's hat, 2 four green pieces of pepper on the pizza, 3 large blue bowl on the right of the picture, 4 red round present, 5 HAPPY written above BIRTHDAY on the card.

TRACK 30

*Part Five. Listen and look at the picture. There is one example.*

**FCH:** Look at this picture!
**M:** Yes, it's Tom the cat's birthday.
**FCH:** He's cooked a pizza for his birthday tea.
**M:** That's right. But look. He's not a very good cook.
**FCH:** Why not?
**M:** The base of the pizza is black. Do you want to colour it?
**FCH:** OK.

*Can you see the black on the pizza base? This is an example. Now you listen and colour and write.*

1
**M:** Do you want to write something in the picture?
**FCH:** Yes! Can I write on Tom's hat?
**M:** Of course. Write COOK on it.
**FCH:** OK! That means someone who makes meals, doesn't it?
**M:** That's right.
**FCH:** OK. I've done that now.
**M:** Good!
2
**FCH:** What are those things on top of the pizza?
**M:** Do you mean the tomatoes?
**FCH:** No. The four things that are long and thin.
**M:** I think those are pieces of pepper.
**FCH:** Right. What colour can we make them?
**M:** What about green?
**FCH:** OK. That's a good colour.
3
**M:** Tom's got salad to eat with his pizza. Can you see the bowl?
**FCH:** Which one? The small one on the left of the picture?
**M:** No, the big one on the right. Do you want to colour it?
**FCH:** Yes, please.
**M:** OK. Let's make it a nice blue colour.
**FCH:** Right. I'm doing that now.
4
**M:** Can you see Tom's presents?
**FCH:** Yes, he's got lots! He's a lucky cat!
**M:** Yes. Why don't you colour one of the presents red?
**FCH:** Which one?
**M:** The round one, I think.
**FCH:** OK. That looks nice.
5
**M:** Tom's got some birthday cards.
**FCH:** Yes. I think they're from his friends.
**M:** And he's writing one with his tail.
**FCH:** Oh, yes. What's he writing?
**M:** I think it says 'Happy Birthday'. Can you finish writing it for him?
**FCH:** OK. What a nice birthday!

## Reading & Writing Part 1 (10 marks): page 111

**Key:** 1 plates, 2 meals, 3 fur, 4 paper, 5 glass, 6 salt, 7 gold, 8 a knife, 9 a scarf, 10 spoons.

## Reading & Writing Part 2 (5 marks): page 112

**Key:** 1 E, 2 G, 3 B, 4 D, 5 H.

## Reading & Writing Part 3 (6 marks): page 113

**Key:** 1 taste, 2 look, 3 soft, 4 sound, 5 terrible, 6 A new person in the family.

## Reading & Writing Part 4 (10 marks): page 114

**Key:** 1 because, 2 to, 3 make, 4 you, 5 an, 6 in, 7 with, 8 one, 9 take, 10 your.

## Reading & Writing Part 5 (7 marks): page 115

**Key:** 1 museum, 2 an animal, 3 excited, 4 materials, 5 six/6 boxes, 6 paper cups. 7 plastic knives.

## Reading & Writing Part 6 (5 marks): page 116

**Key:** 1 so//and, 2 in, 3 made//mixed, 4 it//the dough, 5 was//tasted.

## Reading & Writing Part 7 (5 marks): page 117

**Key:** Pupils' own answers

## Speaking: pages 118–120.

- Part 1. See general notes (page 6) in the introduction for how to set up this part of the Speaking test. Give an example. Aim to elicit six differences from the pupil.
- Part 2. See general notes. Start by introducing John. Say *This is John with his sister, Katy, in the kitchen. I don't know anything about John but you do. I'm going to ask you some questions. What is John making?* Ask the pupils to answer all the questions about John, then say *Now you ask me questions about Katy.* Point to the prompts on the Pupil's card.
- Part 3. See general notes. Start the story *It's the twentieth of January and it's Betty and Daisy's mum's birthday.*
- Part 4. Follow on the theme of birthdays by asking *When's your birthday? What presents do you like? What do you eat on your birthday? Do you like parties? What did you do for your last birthday?*

# Test Units 7-8 pp 121-135

## Listening Part 1 (5 marks): page 121

**Key:** Lines should be drawn as follows:
1 Betty and tall girl standing in striped team's goal
2 Daisy and girl looking at butterfly on her glove
3 Jane and girl with long hair in her eyes
4 Paul and boy with dog
5 William and boy fallen down on ice by piece of wood

TRACK 31

*Part One. Look at the picture. Listen and look. There is one example.*

**M:** I've never played ice hockey. It looks fun.
**FCH:** Yes. My friends love it. And Alex is the best.
**M:** Which boy is he?
**FCH:** He's in front of the goal in a striped sweater.
**M:** What's he doing?
**FCH:** He's hitting the puck (that's like the ball in ice hockey). I think he's going to get a point.

*Can you see the line? This is an example. Now you listen and draw lines.*

**M:** Is your friend Betty playing?
**FCH:** Yes. She's in the striped team too. She's the very tall girl.
**M:** Is she in the other goal?
**FCH:** Yes, she is. She's the best goalkeeper the striped team has ever had.
**M:** And who's that girl? She isn't playing!
**FCH:** The girl who's pulling her sock up?
**M:** No, the one who's looking at her glove.
**FCH:** Oh. That's Daisy.

**M:** What's she doing?
**FCH:** She's looking at a butterfly! She's always dreaming.
**M:** Is your friend Jane here?
**FCH:** Yes, she is. But I don't think she's playing very well.
**M:** How do you know?
**FCH:** Because she's got really long hair and it's dropping in her eyes! She can't see.
**M:** Does she wear glasses sometimes?
**FCH:** Yes, but she's not wearing them now. She doesn't wear them when she's playing ice hockey.
**M:** Good idea. It's very dangerous.
**M:** Ha ha! Look! There's a dog on the ice!
**FCH:** Oh no! Where did it come from?
**M:** I don't know, but that boy is having problems with it!
**FCH:** Oh, that's Paul. I think he's trying to take it back to his dad but he's not very good at skating.
**FCH:** Oh, no! William's fallen over!
**M:** Where?
**FCH:** He's there on the left. I think there's some rubbish on the ice. Is it a piece of wood?
**M:** Oh yes. Do you think he's going to be OK?
**FCH:** I hope so! He's the best player on that team!

## Listening Part 2 (5 marks): page 122

**Key:** 1 twelve//12, 2 Charter, 3 science, 4 five//5, 5 frogs.

TRACK 32

*Part Two. Listen and look. There is one example.*

**F:** Welcome to the library.
**MCH:** Thank you.
**F:** Now, I'd like to ask you a few questions for your library card. Let's start with your name.
**MCH:** It's David Richards.
**F:** Can you spell Richards, please?
**MCH:** Yes, it's R-I-C-H-A-R-D-S.
**F:** Thank you.

*Can you see the answer? Now you listen and write.*

**F:** Now, David. I need to know your age.
**MCH:** OK. Now or next week? It's my birthday on Sunday.
**F:** I see. Let's write your age next week.
**MCH:** I'm going to be 12. I've just started a new school.
**F:** OK. And I need the name of your school, please.
**MCH:** OK. It's Charter Road School.
**F:** Can you spell it for me, please?
**MCH:** Yes, it's C-H-A-R-T-E-R. Charter.
**F:** Thanks.
**F:** And now we have to write your favourite school subject. You've got a badminton racket in your bag, so I think you like sport.
**MCH:** Well, I do. But it isn't my favourite. I've come to the library to borrow lots of books about science. That's my favourite subject.
**F:** OK. And how many books do you want every month?
**MCH:** Well, in the holidays, I read about eight books a month but when I'm at school I haven't got time for so many.
**F:** Mm. OK. Well, let's put five.
**MCH:** That sounds good.
**F:** Right. What kind of book do you want today?
**MCH:** Well, I'm doing a project for the school ezine. I want to write about the tree frogs in South America.
**F:** That's lucky. We've had a new book about them this week.
**MCH:** Great.

## Listening Part 3 (5 marks): page 123

**Key:** 1 D Katy and swimming, 2 H Anna and skiing, 3 C John and athletics, 4 A Lucy and basketball, 5 B Michael and climbing.

TRACK 33

*Part Three. Listen and look. There is one example. What sports are the children good at?*

**M:** Mrs Sims, a lot of children in the school are good at sport. Shall we give out some class sports prizes this year?
**F:** That sounds like a good idea, Mr Jakes.
**M:** What sports do the children in your class enjoy?
**F:** Well, Nick loves sailing. Did you know he's been in a world competition with his father?
**M:** Wow! That's fantastic.

*Can you see the letter F next to Nick? Now you listen and write a letter in each box.*

**M:** And what about his sister, Katy? Is she good at a sport?
**F:** Yes. All her family are good at sport but her favourite is swimming. She goes to the pool in town every morning before school. She's won four gold medals.
**M:** Really? That's wonderful.
**M:** Now what about Anna? She lived in Canada, is she good at snowboarding?
**F:** Yes, but her best sport is skiing. She can go downhill very fast. She always finishes first.
**M:** Who else is there? Oh yes, John! What can he do?
**F:** He's *really* good at athletics. He's won six prizes at his club for the high jump. His mum says he jumps over things at home too! He can't stop!
**M:** We've got a volleyball team in the school. Is anyone in your class good at that? Lucy's good at playing ball games.
**F:** Yes. But she's good at basketball. She's the best player in my class. She's very good at scoring goals and she can run fast.
**M:** Now what about Michael?
**F:** Well, he's terrible at most sports! But he's good at climbing. He's in a club and he often goes up mountains with his father in the holidays.
**M:** Well, all the children in your class sound fantastic. Why don't we give them all a prize?
**F:** Great!

## Listening Part 4 (5 marks): page 124

**Key:** 1 B, 2 C, 3 A, 4 B, 5 A.

TRACK 34

*Part Four. Listen and look. There is one example.*

*Which museum did Sarah go to?*

**M:** Hello Sarah! How was your school trip to the museum? Did you see lots of beautiful art?
**FCH:** We didn't go there, Grandpa.
**M:** Oh. Where did you go?
**FCH:** Well, I wanted to go to a museum and learn about music but we went to the science museum.

*Can you see the tick? Now you listen and tick the box.*

1 *How did Sarah travel to the museum?*
**M:** How did you get there?
**FCH:** It's a long way. It's too far to walk. And my mum couldn't take me and my friends there in her car because she was busy. We went on the school bus.

**2** *How long did it take to get to the museum?*
**M:** How long did it take?
**FCH:** It was really slow. It took one and a half hours!
**M:** Why?
**FCH:** Well, it only took half an hour to get from the school to the town. But there was a cycling competition near the museum. There were lots of people on bicycles! So the last part took *one* hour!

**3** *What did Sarah see at the museum?*
**M:** So what did you see in the museum? The computer section? It's wonderful!
**FCH:** No. That was closed.
**M:** Oh dear. So where did you go? To the dinosaurs?
**FCH:** Some people from my class went there but my friends and I went to see the snakes.

**4** *Why did Sarah fall?*
**M:** Did you have a nice time?
**FCH:** Not really. I had an accident.
**M:** Oh no! What happened?
**FCH:** Well, I was walking through the museum when I fell over.
**M:** Are you sure no one pushed you?
**FCH:** No, there was some water on the floor. My friends thought I was playing. So they started to laugh at me.
**M:** Oh dear!

**5** *What did the museum send to Sarah?*
**M:** Did anyone from the museum say sorry?
**FCH:** Yes. They sent me a card the next day. It was beautiful! It had a picture of a bat on it.
**M:** That's good.
**FCH:** And they sent me two tickets to go again next month.
**M:** Are you going to go?
**FCH:** Yes. Would you like to come with me, Grandpa?
**M:** Yes, please!

## Listening Part 5 (5 marks): page 125

**Key:** 1 a green fish on the grass, 2 a yellow bird in the sky, 3 PICNICS written on the sign on the trunk of tree, above 'here', 4 PAPER written on the rubbish bin on the tree, 5 a blue plastic bag with sun cream next to it.

TRACK 35

*Part Five. Listen and look at the picture. There is one example.*
**F:** The children are having a nice picnic in this picture.
**MCH:** Can I colour it?
**F:** OK. What do you want to colour first?
**MCH:** Can you see the cows in the field?
**F:** Yes.
**MCH:** I'm going to colour the one that's sitting down.
**F:** What colour are you going to do it?
**MCH:** I'm going to colour it black.

*Can you see the black cow? This is an example. Now you listen and colour and write.*

**1**
**F:** The two boys are fishing in the river.
**MCH:** Shall I colour one of the fish? That one's very beautiful.
**F:** Which one?
**MCH:** The one on the grass with a spotted tail.
**F:** OK. Colour that one green.
**MCH:** Right.
**2**
**MCH:** I'm going to colour a bird now.
**F:** Which one? The one in the tree?
**MCH:** No. The one that's flying. Look at its big wings.
**F:** What colour are you going to do it?
**MCH:** Yellow, I think.
**F:** OK. That's a great colour.
**3**
**F:** Do you want to write something now?
**MCH:** OK. What shall I write?
**F::** Can you see the piece of paper on the tree?
**MCH:** Yes, I can. It's under the bird and above the bin.
**F:** That's right. Can you write PICNICS on it?
**MCH:** Yes, OK. That's where people can do that.
**F:** Right!
**4**
**MCH:** There isn't any rubbish in the picture, is there?
**F:** No. Everyone has put it in the bins.
**MCH:** What do you think is in the one on the tree?
**F:** I think it's for paper. Why don't you write PAPER on it?
**MCH:** OK. Good idea.
**5**
**MCH:** The children have got some plastic bags.
**F:** Yes. One of them's got the food in it.
**MCH:** I'm going to colour the other one, I think. It's got some sun cream next to it.
**F:** OK. Colour that bag blue.
**MCH:** Right. I've finished. This is a really good picture.

## Reading & Writing Part 1 (10 marks): page 126

**Key:** 1 spots, 2 picnics, 3 rubbish, 4 sledging, 5 bottles, 6 butterflies, 7 endangered species, 8 summer, 9 striped, 10 athletics.

## Reading & Writing Part 2 (5 marks): page 127

**Key:** 1 G, 2 A, 3 E, 4 H, 5 D.

## Reading & Writing Part 3 (6 marks): page 128

**Key:** 1 wear, 2 cream, 3 forgot, 4 hurting, 5 walk, 6 Listen to your mother.

## Reading & Writing Part 4 (10 marks): page 129

**Key:** 1 protecting, 2 For, 3 who, 4 the, 5 about, 6 die, 7 near, 8 in, 9 than, 10 are.

## Reading & Writing Part 5 (7 marks): page 130

**Key:** 1 the grass, 2 hungry, 3 a (loud) noise//the/a bull, 4 a tree, 5 field, 6 see, 7 (the colour) red.

## Reading & Writing Part 6 (5 marks): page 131

**Key:** 1 went, 2 ever, 3 at, 4 On//Last, 5 like//love//enjoy.

## Reading & Writing Part 7 (5 marks): page 132

**Key:** Pupils' own answers

## Speaking: pages 133–135

- Part 1. See general notes (page 6) in the introduction for how to set up this part of the Speaking test. Give an example. Aim to elicit six differences from the pupil.
- Part 2. See general notes. Start by introducing Tom. Say *This is Tom. He's at the Sports Club party. I don't know anything about him but you do. I'm going to ask you some questions. What sport does Tom play?* Get the pupils to answer all the questions about Tom, then say *Now you ask me questions about Sarah.* Point to the prompts on the Pupil's card.
- Part 3. See general notes. Start the story *It's Robert's birthday today and he's nine years old. He's very happy.*
- Part 4. Follow on the sport and seasons theme by asking *Do you play any sports? What sports do you play? Does your family watch sport on TV? Do you like the winter or the summer best? Why? What new sport would you like to try?*